THE
FAIRTAX
SOLUTION

FINANCIAL JUSTICE FOR
ALL AMERICANS **THE**
FAIRTAX
SOLUTION

Ken Hoagland

SENTINEL

SENTINEL
Published by the Penguin Group
Penguin Group (USA) Inc., 375 Hudson Street,
New York, New York 10014, U.S.A .
Penguin Group (Canada), 90 Eglinton Avenue East, Suite 700, Toronto, Ontario, Canada M4P 2Y3
(a division of Pearson Penguin Canada Inc.)
Penguin Books Ltd, 80 Strand, London WC2R 0RL, England
Penguin Ireland, 25 St. Stephen's Green, Dublin 2, Ireland (a division of Penguin Books Ltd)
Penguin Books Australia Ltd, 250 Camberwell Road, Camberwell, Victoria 3124, Australia
(a division of Pearson Australia Group Pty Ltd)
Penguin Books India Pvt Ltd, 11 Community Centre, Panchsheel Park, New Delhi - 110 017, India
Penguin Group (NZ), 67 Apollo Drive, Rosedale, North Shore 0632, New Zealand
(a division of Pearson New Zealand Ltd)
Penguin Books (South Africa) (Pty) Ltd, 24 Sturdee Avenue, Rosebank, Johannesburg 2196,
South Africa

Penguin Books Ltd, Registered Offices: 80 Strand, London WC2R ORL, England

First published in 2010 by Sentinel,
a member of Penguin Group (USA) Inc.

1   3   5   7   9   10   8   6   4   2

Data for charts from Americans for Fair Taxation

Library of Congress Cataloging-in-Publication Data

Hoagland, Ken.
    The FairTax solution : financial justice for all Americans / Ken Hoagland.
        p.   cm.
    ISBN 978-1-59523-060-7
    1. Sales tax—United States.   2. Spendings tax—United States.   3. Income tax—United States.
I. Title.
    HJ5715.U6H63   2010
    336.200973—dc22   2009039991

Printed in the United States of America
Set in Janson Text
Designed by Neuwirth & Associates, Inc.

There is one special group of people to whom I owe grateful recognition: my beautiful and supportive family.

Brilliant Jack at fourteen, irrepressible Henry at seven, and unusually patient wife, Wendy, have all supported too many hours away, too many long workdays and sleepless nights, and a lot of dinner table talk about the big and little ideas that underlie the FairTax.

Thank you Hoagland family for supporting me just as the families of other volunteers have supported them.

CONTENTS

INTRODUCTION

> "No Capitation or other direct tax shall be laid, unless in Proportion to the Census of Enumeration, hereinbefore, directed to be taken."
>
> —Constitution of the United States, article 1, section 9

THERE IS NOTHING, Benjamin Franklin once noted, more certain than death and taxes. But does our tax system have to lead to national economic death? Many believe that the modest 1912 proposal to "soak the rich" by taxing their income, as originally prohibited by the Constitution, has grown into an overwhelming, self-perpetuating monster that threatens not just average citizens' peace of mind and business owners' best practices but the very foundations of both our economy and our system of democracy.

There is a better way. This book explores the damaging effects of the income-tax system on our economy, examines the bipartisan Washington, D.C., "fortress" of self-interest that protects the system, and suggests a much better way to collect the same amount of federal tax revenues through a national retail consumption tax called the FairTax. It also takes a hard look at why this better public policy can't be achieved unless Americans from across the political spectrum come together to force this fundamental change on Washington.

Basically, the FairTax eliminates the main problem with our current income-tax system by replacing taxes levied on what goes *into* our economy—work, savings, and investment—with taxes taken from what comes *out* of the economy—consumption. This new tax system promises a fresh era of economic growth, elimination of federal taxes on the poor, an end to congressional corruption of the tax code, and ultimately, a far better and more honest relationship between American citizens and their national government.

The FairTax is not new. It is a single-rate, federal retail sales tax collected at the final point of purchase of new goods and services for personal consumption. It has been developed through extensive research over the past fifteen years by some of the most respected economists in the nation. It is a paradigm- and politics-shifting economic proposal first introduced as legislation in 1999 and now pending in Congress with more than fifty congressional cosponsors. If the FairTax legislation passes, the Sixteenth Amendment, which allows the income tax, will be repealed under companion legislation.

For the most part, Washington insiders hate the idea, and citizens who know it love it. Can American citizens, who the framers of the Constitution believed should hold power over their own government, overcome the narrow self-interests of the relatively small but powerful political class who profit so richly from the income-tax system? Can ordinary voters acting together force a change away from an unsustainable and seemingly unstoppable path of government debt? These are the questions that determine whether the FairTax, an "outsider" proposal, can ever become law. The FairTax campaign is as much about the power of the majority in our modern nation as it is about a better national tax system.

If citizens can prevail over the political elite who profit so richly from the complications of the tax code, the FairTax can't come a moment too soon. The nation has taken a path of increasing and damaging public debt larger than at any other time in our history. The magnitude of borrowing and spending is politically possible only because the cost is largely hidden from each of us in taxes withheld from our paychecks and hidden from plain view. It is a dangerous moment for Americans as our government, like a stage performer spinning plates, tries to balance huge new debts, ballooning entitlement spending, and an unprecedented printing of currency by the Federal Reserve.

In essence, because local, state, and national debt is eventually paid by taxpayers out of their earnings, our governments have been running up charges on taxpayer-funded "credit cards." To satisfy government borrowing, each American household now owes foreign and domestic creditors hundreds of thousands of dollars. In our discussion of the FairTax, we will explore how the FairTax can bring federal spending into the open so that Americans can first see how it affects their own earnings and then regain their deserved voice in such decisions.

The "full faith and credit" of the United States really means that our elected officials have pledged part of the earnings of Americans—both now and in the future—to satisfy debt obligations. When the nation sells treasury notes to China, for example, or when your city or local school district raises funds through bond sales, they are selling interest-bearing IOUs with the promise that you and your fellow citizens will pay the mounting interest charges and satisfy the loans by giving up a part of your work earnings, your savings, and your investments. Every year sees new taxpayer debt added to the old.

In 2008 *USA Today* reported that the debt undertaken by the American government at just the national level totaled a mind-boggling $546,668 per household. The debt entered into by our federal government amounts to four times what the average U.S. household owes for all mortgages, car loans, credit cards, and other debt combined. "We have a huge implicit mortgage on every household in America—except, unlike a real mortgage, it's not backed up by a house," said David Walker, former U.S. comptroller general, in the article. Instead, those debts are based on government promises that the American people will pay back every penny loaned to us, plus interest.

That mountain of debt just keeps getting larger. In 2008 alone, the federal government incurred $6.8 trillion in new debt, pushing the total owed to a record $63.8 trillion. In 2009, almost two trillion dollars of debt was added, and every year for the next ten years, the federal government will add at least a trillion dollars of new debt. At some point it is fair—and incredibly important—to ask whether such obligations are actually helping Americans or making our "pursuit of happiness" much harder.

When Ronald Reagan became president in 1980, government, consumer, and business debt amounted to a little over 90 percent of the gross domestic product, or the national wealth produced annually. During the Great Depression, our darkest economic hour, our collective debt totaled just over 250 percent of the GDP. By 2008, we owed more than 350 percent of all the wealth created in the nation that year.

Paradoxically and self-destructively, our income-tax system encourages deeper personal and government debt, punishes wealth, taxes the hiring of new workers and every successful investment and, worst of all, hides the cost of government spending from the American people who pay the bill.

> *The FairTax is really three things—a better national tax system, a direct path out of our fiscal mess, and the means to reconnect the will of the majority to the behavior of our government.*

Chapter 1   **What Is the FairTax?**

> "Would it not be better to simplify the system of taxation rather than to spread it over such a variety of subjects, and pass the money through so many new hands?"
> —**Thomas Jefferson to James Madison**

I T'S A VERY GOOD idea for each of us to ask the same question that Jefferson posed to Madison, because the income tax is a complicated, ineffective, and intrusive system that threatens the very American dream the Founders hoped to foster in our new nation. The FairTax simplifies tax collection, makes crystal clear the cost of government, puts tax decisions into the hands of individuals, and removes a huge drag on our economy and future growth.

The FairTax is a nonregressive national retail consumption tax. Instead of taxing our earnings, the FairTax raises taxes at the point of final retail sale of goods and services for personal consumption. We pay our national taxes at the cash register throughout the year, and those who spend more pay more taxes. Under the FairTax the IRS is dismantled and relegated to the history books. Through the FairTax's unique design the poor are protected and the system is more progressive and far fairer than the income-tax system.

Federal taxes under the FairTax plan are paid by every consumer at the cash register, but only at the point of final retail sale. To eliminate the double, triple, and even quadruple taxation we now suffer, used goods are not subject to the FairTax. For every purchase of new goods and services, the retailer collects 23 percent of the sum of the price of the goods or services and the tax amount. Expressed as sales taxes are usually calculated, the retailer collects 30 percent of the price of the goods or services (I'll explain more about "inclusive/exclusive" calculations later). These funds are then remitted to the U.S. Treasury Department through state sales tax authorities. The retailer keeps a quarter of 1 percent of the collected taxes for its trouble.

The FairTax replaces the entire range of income-based taxes, eliminating the personal income tax, all federal business taxes, the "inheritance tax," the Social Security and Medicare payroll taxes, the capital-gains tax on savings and investments, and even the marriage penalty and the Alternative Minimum Tax. Because consumption is a broader base for taxes than earnings, the FairTax raises exactly the same amount of revenue as all of these other taxes with an evenly applied national retail sales tax that is collected through existing state sales-tax networks.

Under the FairTax the expensive and frustrating annual headache of filing complicated personal tax forms ends forever. Because the FairTax is levied without exception on all new goods and services, the rules for compliance are simple and straightforward. It is simplicity itself, unlike the endless maze of exemptions, deductions, and confusing rules that make "tax *code*" an especially apt name.

The FairTax ends the original bad idea of direct taxation of earnings, savings, and investment and replaces the revenue, penny for penny, with a tax on retail sales. The natio. is expanded to include the nearly $2 trillion–a–year ground" economy, millions of illegal immigrants who be taxpayers as consumers, and all those who have found w. legal and illegal, to avoid paying billions of dollars in taxes. No American any longer needs an expert to tell them what they owe in taxes, and the connection between what our government spends and what we pay out of our own earnings for government spending comes into the open with every retail purchase.

Very importantly, the FairTax changes the upside-down definition of whether our earnings belong first to the federal government or first to each citizen. It gives us back control over our earnings by ending federal withholding of taxes from our paychecks and by doing this, shifts tax decisions away from Congress to individuals in their personal consumption choices. Because no national taxes are withheld from workers' paychecks under the FairTax, take-home pay increases dramatically. Under the FairTax what we earn belongs first to us, with our personal consumption choices defining how much federal tax we pay and when. The FairTax also corrects the many distortions inherent in the income-tax system—or in provisions added by Congress over nearly a century—that do serious damage to our economy.

Significantly, the FairTax ends what has made the original terrible idea of direct taxation even worse—nearly one hundred years of congressional and lobbyist tinkering that has transformed, complicated, and corrupted what was originally a relatively simple and modest tax on the wealthy into 67,500 pages of almost indecipherable tax regulations that now intrude into the life of every American. Because there are no exceptions in the FairTax, congressional committees that now routinely grant

ax lobbyists seeking favors on behalf of the
re dealt out of manipulating the new fed-

nt to shift to a new way of collecting na-
ble answer to this question is that the cur-
lly broken and needs to be fixed. It's not
April 15; the income-tax system actually
works against the American economy, and the damage has been
compounded by the army of tax lobbyists who, over the past
near century, have found a willing partner in Congress. The
FairTax is not "reform" but *replacement* of the broken federal
tax system.

Under the income-tax system, debt is more favorable than
wealth (you can write off debt and interest payments on debt),
upward mobility is punished as more taxes are levied at each
rung up the financial ladder, every new business success is hob-
bled by higher taxes, regressive taxes keep the poor down, and
the hiring of new employees costs businesses not just wages and
benefits but employment taxes.

Adding insult to injury, married Americans pay higher taxes
than singles, the same income is subject to double and triple taxation (ask any senior who sees his or her Social Security benefits
taxed), and foreign businesses enjoy a price advantage over American producers because of our tax code. The income-tax concept
collects federal revenues by taxing American productivity—a terrible mistake when first enacted that has only become more pronounced since 1912. Simply put, the FairTax fixes all the problems
inherent in the income-tax system.

Under the FairTax, federal taxes are paid at the cash register—
and every consumer pays his or her fair share in a highly visible,
simple and transparent system. Normally, sales taxes are unfair
to those with less because they spend a larger percentage of what

they earn on the basic necessities of life and therefore spend a larger percentage of their income on sales taxes than those with more wealth. Unlike any other sales tax, however, the FairTax protects the poor and middle class from regressivity by building in a monthly 100 percent reimbursement on spending up to the poverty level and entirely eliminating highly regressive Social Security and Medicare payroll taxes.

This monthly payment, called a prebate, is calculated based on family size, not income, and is paid to every household at the first of each month, so every American benefits. The prebate helps the middle class tremendously, but those at the poverty level and below enjoy the most dramatic effects of tax reduction and gains in purchasing power.

Because under the FairTax all personal federal taxes are collected as a retail sales tax, the federal government no longer withholds taxes from American paychecks to fund Medicare and Social Security. This means that take-home pay goes up dramatically. More take-home pay permanently stimulates the consumer economy and provides more discretionary spending that can be devoted to consumption, savings, or investment. Rather than being based solely on what we earn and being automatically deducted from our earnings, federal taxes become a function of personal consumption decisions, allowing us to individually decide the *size and timing* of our tax burden.

When taxes are paid throughout the year when purchasing new goods and services, all individual tax returns are eliminated and April 15 becomes just another spring day. This alone produces an immediate savings of an estimated $300 billion in annual tax-preparation costs. There is no need for tax preparation services because the complicated tax code does not exist under the FairTax. Certified public accountants return to the useful work of helping businesses with the books and growing our wealth and get out of the business of being human seeing eye dogs guiding us through the overwhelming maze of complexity created by our own government.

There are no federal business taxes under the FairTax. In reality, such taxes are only an illusion under the income-tax system because businesses don't really fund these tax costs. Instead, businesses pass along the cost of taxes to consumers and workers by either hiking prices or depressing wages and benefits in order to stay competitive with foreign producers who are not burdened with national taxes on exported products. These embedded tax costs are yet another way that the true cost of our government is hidden from the American taxpayer and consumer and yet another way the income tax system hurts American companies.

The FairTax fixes the destructive effects of embedding hidden tax costs—like corporate taxes and the employer's share of Social Security and Medicare taxes—in the price of American goods and services. These costs make American products less competitive, drive our businesses offshore, and put pressure on American producers to depress wages and benefits.

In addition to eliminating taxes on business profits, the FairTax does not tax anything that goes, wholesale, *into* a business. This means that businesses can make decisions based on growth and on the health of the business instead of on tax consequences. This is a healthy step forward because the income-tax code has introduced destructive and politically driven tax considerations into the "natural selection" forces that should determine business survival and growth. The elimination of federal business taxes will also reduce the cost of producing goods and services in America, and most experts agree that without these taxes, retail prices will be forced down through competitive pressures.

Under the FairTax, every business with retail sales collects and remits the FairTax to the network of state sales-tax authorities that now exist in forty-four states. The other six states—Alaska, Delaware, Hawaii, Montana, New Hampshire, and Oregon—are required to establish sales-tax programs to collect the FairTax.

As I have said, there are no Social Security or Medicare payroll taxes under the FairTax, but because of the FairTax's design, a broader stream of revenue is available to each program than under the current system. Today only FICA (Federal Insurance Contributions Act) tax revenues contribute to Social Security and Medicare payments. Under the FairTax, all tax revenues become equally available to all federal programs, including Social Security and Medicare. The FairTax ends the fiction of a "lockbox" account for Social Security—the idea that the trillions of dollars of taxes we have all paid in have been "saved" by our government for future benefit payments.

Ending this deliberately fostered illusion will allow an honest national discussion about how to save Social Security and Medicare without either bankrupting the coming generations or betraying those who have already paid in so much. While the FairTax can't solve the structural problems of either program, it provides a broader base of funds to these programs and more security to today's retirees until necessary and commonsense solutions are put in place.

Unlike the income-tax system, the FairTax applies equally to every consumer in the United States, including those who today don't report income or who use sophisticated tax strategies to avoid paying what they owe. Illegal immigrants, drug dealers, gamblers, prostitutes, and wealthy "loophole surfers" all become part of the tax base when buying things for personal consumption. Since everyone purchases goods and services, everyone will contribute to the tax base. Under this system, the tax base expands dramatically and loopholes and gimmicks are eliminated, allowing most current taxpayers to pay less. At most, consumers will pay 23 percent of any money they *spend* instead of an average of 30 percent of all the money they *earn*. Most people, in fact, will pay less than 23 percent of total income because it takes a lot of spending to reach that level. The poor, who certainly do generally spend everything they earn just to keep body and soul together, are, by design, protected under the FairTax.

The FairTax collects the same amount of revenue as the income-tax system but spreads the burden more equitably and transparently. By taxing consumption instead of earnings, the FairTax ensures that everyone who consumes contributes, the complex and often arbitrary definitions of "income" disappear, the overly complicated calculations disappear, the loopholes bought and paid for by special interests disappear, and significant taxes now hidden in the price of American goods and services are eliminated. A broader tax base is created; with a contribution required even from the forty million foreign tourists who visit the United States each year.

Helpfully, education costs are considered investments in human capital and are therefore not subject to the FairTax. That means that college costs and all other education costs, including elementary and secondary-school tuition, are paid for with what is now considered pretax income, free of any federal taxation. This is one more way the FairTax puts the nation on a path of growth and economic health.

As the last century has proved, only truly fundamental change can correct the many problems of the income-tax system. Incremental change, even when ambitious, amounts to rearranging deck chairs on a sinking ship doomed by its original design errors. With one cut of the Gordian knot, the FairTax ends the destructive effects of taxes on income along with the equally damaging effects of politics and lobbying profits that now drive the income-tax system in Congress.

Washington insiders have created a monster—a contradictory and arbitrary patchwork of definitions that allows tax favors for "friends" and tax-code punishments of political enemies. Inspired by everything but sound policy, ham-handed congressional attempts to manipulate citizen and business behavior have backfired again and again, costing taxpayers billions of dollars and doing real damage to the national economy. Congressional drafting errors like the failure to index the Alternative Minimum Tax for inflation and unintended consequences like the "marriage penalty," as well as all the other terribly counterproductive effects of our badly broken system, are erased with the FairTax.

The FairTax Rate

Under the FairTax, a 23 percent tax is collected on the retail sale of all new goods and services at the time of purchase. To clarify, that 23 percent is the amount collected on *the sum of two amounts:* the tax and the price of the purchased item. When you go into a shoe store, for example, you might see a $100 price tag on a pair of shoes. That $100 price includes a $23 FairTax that goes to the federal government (minus a small fee paid to the retailer). The other $77 goes to the shoe store. Out of the $100 dollars, you pay a highly visible $23 tax, which is noted on your receipt. To most people this is a 23 percent tax, but others are quick to note that $23 represents 30 percent of a $77 purchase.

If this seems confusing, don't feel alone, because sales-tax rates are usually expressed "exclusive" of the tax amount; in other words, the tax is not part of the total upon which the percentage rate is calculated. If income-tax rates were calculated this way (exclusive of the tax itself), there would be no confusion and the FairTax would be described as a 30 percent retail consumption tax. But, as is doubtless surprising to many, income-tax rates are not calculated this way. Here is how the inclusive income-tax rates would change if calculated exclusively (like sales-tax rates): 15 percent inclusive = 18 percent exclusive; 20 percent inclusive = 25 percent exclusive; 25 percent inclusive = 33 percent exclusive; 33 percent inclusive = 50 percent exclusive; and 50 percent inclusive = 100 percent exclusive.

The FairTax is calculated the same way your income-tax rate is calculated—inclusively. In other words, a 15 percent income-tax bracket really means you pay 15 percent of the total of your taxes and your earnings added together or, put another way, 18 percent of just the earnings amount. The seemingly lower percentage figures of the FairTax rate and income-tax rates result from the inclusive method of calculation, which includes both the tax paid and the earnings amount in a single sum—and then calculates the ratio between the tax and that combined sum.

The "tax-inclusive" FairTax rate of 23 percent simply makes it easier to compare the FairTax rate to current income tax rates. Without stating the rate this way, it would be very difficult for average people to compare the annual cost of the FairTax with what they pay today under the income-tax system. In one sense, the difference between a 23 percent tax-inclusive rate and a 30 percent tax-exclusive rate is similar to the nonexistent difference between measuring an object in centimeters and measuring it in inches— whichever measurement you use, the distance (or tax amount) is the same.

It should be noted that the FairTax only replaces the *federal* tax system, and therefore, state and local taxes still exist under this new system. State sales and income taxes and local property taxes remain as they are, although federal taxes formerly hidden as "embedded" taxes are shifted into the open.

While a 23 percent or 30 percent rate may seem high at first glance, it actually amounts to a lower percentage of income than what most Americans now pay in federal taxes. Under our current system, in addition to income taxes, we pay Social Security and Medicare taxes, embedded taxes added to the price of consumer goods, and the significant cost of compliance with the federal income-tax system. The FairTax eliminates all personal tax-compliance costs.

If you work for an employer, the amount of FICA taxes (for Medicare and Social Security) withheld from your paycheck equals 7.65 percent of your earnings up to about $102,500. Your employer pays an equal amount to the federal government. If you are self-employed, you pay the full freight—15.3 percent— which is why this is sometimes called the "self-employment tax." The FairTax eliminates and replaces these taxes.

Since the FairTax is based on consumption, those who spend more pay more taxes. Those who spend less pay less. Those who purchase only the necessities of life will be compensated by the prebate reimbursement. Because the wealthy typically spend more than lower- or middle-class Americans, they will pay more taxes over the year on their purchases. Because everyone will have more control over their money and more disposable income with increased take-home pay, the FairTax will have a rapid, dramatic, and positive effect on job creation and the overall economy.

Let's look at high-, medium-, and low-income Americans and see how they are treated under the FairTax. When a billionaire spends $10 billion, she pays a tax of $2.3 billion and gets a prebate of $4,697 (assuming she is married and has no children). Her effective tax rate as a percentage of spending is 22.95 percent. If a middle-income married couple with no children *spends* $50,000, they pay $6,803 (net of their prebate), for an effective tax rate of 13.6 percent. The effective tax rate increases as spending increases but *never* exceeds 23 percent. If this same couple *earns* $50,000 in wages today, under the current tax system, they pay $4,093 in income taxes and $3,825 in payroll taxes, for a total of $7,918 in taxes (15.8 percent)—a tax burden significantly higher than under the FairTax. Mr. and Mrs. Middle owe even more than these figures indicate because under the income tax system they pay hidden income tax costs embedded in the price of American-made goods and services every time they make a purchase (which I will discuss a little later in some depth). Finally, under the FairTax, a low-income couple at or below the poverty line who spends everything they earn pays *no net FairTax at all*. Today, under the income-tax system, they not only pay almost 8 percent of earnings in payroll taxes (the employee's share), but they also pay hidden taxes—arising from corporate taxes, private-sector compliance costs, and payroll taxes passed on to consumers and embedded in the price of everything they buy.

The following chart makes clear that this national tax never exceeds 23 percent of spending. But to get to that full level of taxation you would have to spend more than $900,000 on personal consumption! For most Americans, annual tax costs under the FairTax are significantly less than 23 percent.

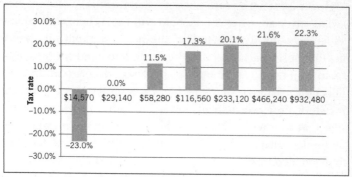

EFFECTIVE FAIRTAX RATE: 2009
Family of four with two children

Source: Americans for Fair Taxation.

The Tax Base Grows Under the FairTax

The tax base will dramatically expand under the FairTax. With more people paying taxes, each taxpayer can carry less of the burden.

The new system collects taxes from the twelve to twenty million illegal immigrants in the United States who currently pay no income taxes at all but who will pay the FairTax on retail purchases as consumers. In addition, the "underground" economy of drug dealers, gamblers, off-the-books workers, and other under-the-table enterprises becomes part of the tax base because, when any of these people makes a purchase—whether it's a handbag or a new speedboat—they will be charged the 23 percent tax like everyone else. This means that the profits derived from gambling, prostitution, drug dealing, and other cash activities now conducted under the table will become part of the national tax base when these profits are spent. The currently untaxed underground economy is estimated to be as large as $2 trillion a year.

The tax base under the FairTax will expand not only to include illegal immigrants and off-the-books workers but also to include those Americans wealthy enough to employ tax lobbyists to gain breaks and loopholes in the current system. In fact, unlike the existing system, the FairTax taxes the existing wealth of millionaires, when spent, instead of current earnings. This solves yet another imbalance in the income tax system whereby the modest salary of a worker is taxed at a higher rate than the dividend income of her millionaire boss. The FairTax equalizes tax treatment, and the prebate and elimination of the FICA payroll tax make the new system much more progressive. Because all tax loopholes will finally close upon enactment of the FairTax, the tax code will be restored to a fair and simple system free of the corrupting effects of power, politics, and profit-driven manipulation.

A close examination of the economy reveals that consumption is a much larger and more stable base for taxation than earnings. The following chart compares the yearly changes in the tax base for the income tax (adjusted gross income, or AGI) and the FairTax (personal-consumption expenditures, or PCE) for the years 1974 to 2004.

Consumption expenditures have steadily grown from year to year, while adjusted gross income dropped from 2000 to 2001 and from 2001 to 2002—two years in a row. The higher growth rates of AGI in boom years result in overspending and then, when the economy slows down, either budget cuts are needed or, as is more often the case, taxes are raised or the budget deficit increases.

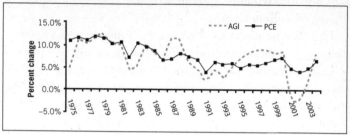

STABILITY OF THE TAX BASE, 1974–2004

Source: Americans for Fair Taxation.

The Prebate

Unlike any other sales tax, the FairTax allows for a "prebate" check to be sent to every American household at the first of each month. This prebate reimburses some or all of the FairTax spent on the necessities of life. In essence, the government "floats" in advance all or part of the tax to be paid by Americans over the next month.

The prebate amount is calculated by family size and reimburses all taxes paid on spending up to the annually adjusted federal poverty-level income. The prebate assumes that those at the poverty level will spend 100 percent of their income on the necessities of life—just keeping body and soul together—and should not pay *any* federal tax on their consumption. Thus, the prebate returns 23 percent of a poverty-level income to every American household. This element of the FairTax plan helps everyone but represents the single greatest public-policy change that can help the poor have a fair chance to escape poverty.

That annually adjusted calculation of the poverty level by family size becomes the benchmark for the monthly prebate amount sent to every American household. The prebate wipes out the FairTax on the poor, dramatically helps the middle class, and means little to Bill Gates, even though he gets one too.

By building into the tax system a universal prebate based on family size instead of income, the progressive nature of the FairTax (meaning the poor are not unfairly penalized with a simple percentage flat tax) is possible without the federal government's being required to know—and check—every penny Americans earn, receive, spend, or invest. Once upon a time that information was considered very personal; under the FairTax it will be again.

To calculate the prebate check amount, a poverty-level income based on family size is multiplied by 23 percent and divided into twelve equal payments. Those payments are sent to every American household once a month. Under this system, nearly all federal taxes on the poor (excise taxes and user fees still exist) are effectively eliminated through this monthly reimbursement.

So why does the check go to Bill Gates and Warren Buffett when they don't need it? Because, at its very core, the FairTax is a shift to a fair and balanced tax system that does not take income into account at all. The FairTax operates on the assumption that millionaires and billionaires consume more than average Americans, and will therefore pay more in taxes. But they are still entitled to the same benefits toward the necessities of life as every other American.

The prebate replaces tax exemptions so that taxes on the necessities of life—bread, milk, house payments and rent, doctor bills, gasoline, and clothing—are reimbursed before the tax is paid—hence the term "prebate." This is *not* a welfare payment but a thirty-day advance of our citizens' own wealth that will be paid that month in consumption taxes to the government. By shifting from the confusing welter of tax treatments for different kinds of spending and earnings under different circumstances to a universal monthly prebate, the FairTax ends the corrupt practices and the ability of Congress to sell off pieces of the tax code to lobbyists and favored constituents.

The universal prebate and elimination of highly regressive FICA payroll taxes makes the FairTax far more "progressive" than the income-tax system. It entirely lifts the burden of regressive FICA taxes from the shoulders of the poor (and everyone else), and it entirely eliminates the weight of federal taxation on earnings. Every worker takes home a paycheck free of all federal withholding and payroll taxes. Every purchase is made with what is today considered "pretax" or "gross" income.

2009 FAIRTAX PREBATE SCHEDULE

Family size	ONE-ADULT HOUSEHOLD Annual Consumption Allowance	Annual Rebate	Monthly Rebate	Family size	TWO-ADULT HOUSEHOLD Annual Consumption Allowance	Annual Rebate	Monthly Rebate
1 person	$10,830	$2,491	$208	Couple	$21,660	$4,982	$415
and 1 child	$14,570	$3,351	$279	and 1 child	$25,400	$5,842	$487
and 2 children	$18,310	$4,211	$351	and 2 children	$29,140	$6,702	$559
and 3 children	$22,050	$5,072	$423	and 3 children	$32,880	$7,562	$630
and 4 children	$25,790	$5,932	$494	and 4 children	$36,620	$8,423	$702
and 5 children	$29,530	$6,792	$566	and 5 children	$40,360	$9,283	$774
and 6 children	$32,270	$7,422	$619	and 6 children	$44,100	$10,143	$845
and 7 children	$37,010	$8,512	$709	and 7 children	$47,840	$11,003	$917

Source: Americans for Fair Taxation.

Chapter 2 **The Effect of the FairTax on the National Economy**

> "A wise and frugal government, which shall restrain
> men from injuring one another, which shall leave them
> otherwise free to regulate their own pursuits of industry
> and improvement, and shall not take from the mouth
> of labor the bread it has earned. This is the sum of
> good government, and this is necessary to close the
> circle of our felicities."
> —**Thomas Jefferson**

TODAY NEARLY ALL American businesses weigh every decision they make against tax consequences. The tax code is such a collection of arbitrary provisions—the result of endless congressional manipulation—that compliance becomes more an expensive art than a science.

And even if we follow the tax code to the letter, by its very nature it punishes us for our success. The phrase "income-tax system" says it all—today we tax the very thing our economy needs to grow—income and that which produces income. We take money from savings, from returns on investment, and from what we are paid for our labor. Shifting away from taxes on income will have an immediate effect on our economic health and prospects for future growth.

When taxes are removed from investment, people are more willing to invest. Additional capital formation leads to higher productivity, research advances, more jobs, and better wages and benefits. This occurs up and down the economic line as individuals save more and invest more, and businesses and large investors freed from hobbling taxes put their wealth to more productive use. The wealth made available under the FairTax system allows faster advances in technology and innovation, expansion of existing businesses, and creation of new ones, leading to a new era of robust growth in our economy. Under the FairTax "a rising sea lifts all boats."

A study by the Government Accountability Office estimated that the federal tax system imposes efficiency costs (expenses that come out of productivity) on the U.S. economy of 2 percent to 5 percent of GDP. It's a huge collective sum devoted to tax preparation and other tax-system costs that should be available for investment and growth. Under the FairTax, average Americans are at least 10 percent and probably 15 percent better off than under the current system within ten years because production costs fall, purchasing power increases, and more jobs are produced. That translates to an increase of $3,000 to $4,500 per household per year.

The FairTax will provide needed medicine for the ailing economy. Economist Dale Jorgenson of Harvard University argues that "the revenue neutral substitution of the FairTax for existing taxes would have an immediate and powerful impact on the level of economic activity. GDP would increase by almost 10.5 percent in the first year." Laurence Kotlikoff of Boston University found that implementation of the proposed tax-reform plan "raises the economy's capital stock by 42 percent, its labor supply by four percent, its output by 12 percent, and its real wage rate by 8 percent. It also lowers real interest rates by more than one quarter."

As the simple chart illustrates, higher take-home wages following the implementation of the FairTax proposal provide an immediate incentive for people to work more. During the first year after implementation, this will lead to total employment growth of 3.5 percent in excess of the baseline scenario (our economic condition *with* the income-tax system). By year ten, employment in the United States will be 9 percent higher than it would be under the current system. This should come as welcome and important news as the nation struggles with a painfully high unemployment rate.

Under the FairTax, total labor income will also increase due to the fact that individuals will take home more of their earnings, a large percentage of which are currently considered pretax. In the first year, total labor income will rise 27.4 percent compared to the baseline. By year ten, labor income will be more than 41 percent higher than it would be under our

CUMULATIVE GROWTH IN EMPLOYMENT, TAKE-HOME WAGES, AND AGGREGATE TAKE-HOME LABOR INCOME DUE TO FAIRTAX PROPOSAL COMPARED TO BASELINE

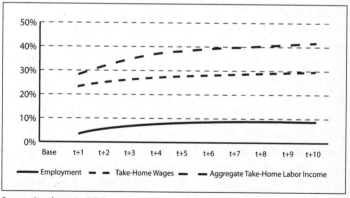

Source: Americans for Fair Taxation.

current system. In simple terms this means far more jobs at higher wages.

The FairTax and Business

Right now America has the second-highest corporate tax rate in the world. We take a significant portion of what businesses earn in profits away from them because we like the idea of making big business "pay its fair share." But it doesn't work that way.

A study by Kevin A. Hassett and Aparna Mathur of the American Enterprise Institute, called "Taxes and Wages" and presented to the House Ways and Means Committee on June 22, 2006, shows that high corporate taxes depress average manufacturing wages. Based on data for seventy countries over twenty-two years, Hassett and Mathur testified that higher corporate tax rates lead to lower wages, with a 1 percent increase in corporate tax rates associated with a 0.7 percent to 0.9 percent drop in wage rates. This implies that if the average domestic corporate tax rate decreased from 35 percent to 25 percent (a 28 percent decrease), average wages would increase by more than 25 percent.

The other common consequence of high business taxes is the shifting of such costs to the consumer through the prices of goods and services. Corporate taxes don't come out of some secret big-business bank account or the CEO's salary, but frequently out of consumers' pockets. This is also where corporations find the funds for their Social Security and Medicare contributions and incredibly high tax-compliance costs. In order to remain profitable, businesses jack up their prices so the tax burden is thrust onto the consumer. This not only affects the price of our products but also stifles job creation because higher prices make American companies far less competitive with foreign producers.

When the FairTax is enacted, competitive pressures will certainly drive down retail prices. Here's why. Let's imagine that American voters have finally thrown off the income-tax system in favor of the FairTax. Pepsi and Coca-Cola suddenly find that the cost of producing their products has dropped substantially. Coca-Cola decides to keep the extra money and reward shareholders with larger dividends. Pepsi, on the other hand, sees an opportunity to gain an edge in the market and drops the price of its product. A year later, Coca-Cola shareholders are demanding answers: Why has the market share of Coca-Cola shrunk? Why has the stock price declined?

The answer is plain: when consumers go to the soft-drink machine or grocery store, some choose the less expensive brand. These kinds of competitive pressures will work throughout the economy to reduce retail prices or address the other effect of embedded tax costs: decreased wages and benefits. Unlike the income tax, the FairTax exacts no tax "penalty" when a company decides to hire new employees or increase wages and benefits to keep valued employees in order to grow and stay competitive.

By eliminating these costs, the FairTax removes the strong incentive for American-based companies to shelter profits overseas by relocating operations to more favorable tax environments. Lower labor costs and easier environmental regulations already act as an offshore magnet on American producers. Since we can't dictate how foreign governments and economies operate, our only hope to entice foreign-based businesses here and bring American businesses back home is to fix the broken tax system. Research shows that we can do exactly that with the FairTax.

The Big-Business Straw Man

"When there is an income tax, the just man will pay more and the unjust less on the same amount of income."
— PLATO

In recent decades, it's become popular and easy for politicians to blame business as the bad guys. To gain votes, candidates and elected officials like to exploit our natural indignation over the impersonality of modern life—poor customer service, high prices, layoffs, and in some cases, outright predatory and irresponsible behavior, as well as Plato's warning thousands of years ago. What these politicians fail to note is that commerce, productivity, and pure and applied research, not government spending, make the high standard of living in the United States possible. Taking money away from business so government has more money to spend is like selling the horses to invest in the stables.

We sometimes overlook the truth that the retirement income of teachers, the wages of parents, the taxes that allow us to build parks and libraries, and funding for the national defense come from the risks and rewards of the people who create and manage our businesses. One need not jettison indignation over the behavior of bad players like Enron or Countrywide Mortgage to recognize that business drives opportunity and the creation of both personal and national wealth. The indignation we feel about bad business practices is commonly exploited to justify taking more money from the private sector. This is a bad bargain for the American people and bad for our job prospects and global competitiveness in the future.

The "shocking" revelation that American businesses are sheltering their profits overseas and far away from the second-highest corporate tax rate in the world (Japan's is first) comes as a surprise to no one but those *feigning* surprise for political gain. According to the Joint Committee on Taxation, the failure to tax the foreign income of U.S.-controlled corporations will cost the government almost $56 billion between 2008 and 2012. Who can blame these companies for keeping their profits away from our corrupted tax code and the sweaty, outstretched hands of members of Congress and Washington tax lobbyists?

In some parts of the world, the bribe to gain government favor is a common, even if illegal, transaction. Here in the United States, political contributions to those on tax-writing committees, fees to tax lobbyists, lunches, trips, and other inducements are accepted and governed by "ethics" rules. Such inducements to grant favors are not only legal but the basis of a thriving lobby business inside Washington's beltway. More than half of the $2.5 billion spent annually on lobbying in Washington is spent in pursuit of "favors" in the income tax code. This has sadly and wrongly come to be seen as nothing more than the cost of doing business in the United States.

When politicians promise to "close business loopholes," they really mean that some past favors are being rescinded and a new feeding frenzy of lobbying activity for new favors is about to begin. It's all part of the corrupted tax code that makes members of Congress from both parties very powerful and lobbyists very wealthy and that does real damage to the American economy. Unfortunately, this is one activity that sees true bipartisan cooperation among the power elite in Washington.

By shifting away from the income-tax system, the natural appetite of business to grow larger, make more profits, and prosper will be unleashed, and as a result, our economy will benefit.

Under the FairTax, every business prospers or fails based solely on how the company is run and how the marketplace is faring—not on arbitrary and politically driven additions to the tax system. The FairTax also offers compelling advantages to small businesses, not just large corporations who can afford to game the income-tax code. According to the Tax Foundation, small businesses spend an astounding $724 in compliance costs for every $100 they pay in income tax. More than 90 percent of all U.S. corporations have assets of $1 million or less and, therefore, collectively carry a tax-compliance cost that is about twenty-seven times greater than that of the largest U.S. corporations, those with $10 billion or more in assets.

Many experts predict an almost immediate $10–15 trillion infusion of private investment, now offshore, into the American economy because of elimination of the corporate income tax. They say that the United States will become the tax haven to the world because the FairTax is a far superior system to anything now in existence and because foreign-based businesses will rush to relocate here, the only "tax free manufacturing zone" to be closer to the world's largest consumer economy.

According to remarks by former House Ways and Means chairman Bill Archer, one study, conducted at Princeton University and commissioned by the Ways and Means Committee, surveyed the five hundred largest foreign corporations doing business in the United States and asked—after explaining how the FairTax worked—what it would mean to these companies. Eight out of ten answered that they would either move their headquarters here or build their next major subsidiary here. That response should come as little surprise. The United States has the richest consumer market in the world. It is America's tax policies that keep more investment from our shores.

Every dollar invested and every new business relocated here would create more jobs for Americans, healthy competition for needed American workers, and growth in the national economy. With unemployment rates so painfully high across the nation right now, the FairTax provides the most direct route to a full economic recovery by stimulating job creation and wage growth.

As part of the more than $20 million worth of economic research spent over the last decade on the FairTax, the Beacon Hill Institute at Boston University undertook advanced economic modeling of the FairTax to examine its future effects on our economy. The results promise welcome growth and a way out of the worst recession since the Great Depression.

Beacon Hill used its established computable general equilibrium (CGE) model to estimate the effects of the FairTax on income, employment, wages, etc., compared to what these indicators would be if the current tax system remained in place.

Here is a snapshot of the major findings:

- GDP would be 7.9 percent higher in the first year, 10.9 percent higher in year ten, and 10.3 percent higher in year twenty-five after enactment of the FairTax than it would be if the current system remained in place.
- Domestic investment (the amount of money invested back into American businesses and research) would be 74.5 percent higher, 75.9 percent higher, and 65.2 percent higher in years one, ten, and twenty-five, respectively.
- Capital stock (all shares of existing publicly traded companies) would be 9.3 percent higher in year five, 14.1 percent higher in year ten, and 17.3 percent higher in year twenty-five.
- Real wages would be 10.3 percent, 9.5 percent, and 9.2 percent higher in years one, ten, and twenty-five, respectively.
- Consumption would drop slightly in the first two years (0.6 percent and 0.8 percent) and then rebound to 1.8

percent higher in year five, 4.3 percent higher in year ten, and 6 percent higher in year twenty-five.

The findings for 2007 through 2031 are summarized in the table below. The table shows the percentage difference in each indicator resulting from implementation of the FairTax for selected years from 2007 to 2031. For example, real GDP would be 7.9 percent higher in 2007 under the FairTax than under the "benchmark" (current law) and 10.3 percent higher by 2031.

SUMMARY OF EFFECTS OF THE FAIRTAX RELATIVE TO CURRENT LAW, 2007–2031 (PERCENT CHANGE)

Year	2007	2008	2009	2010	2011	2016	2021	2026	2031
Period	1	2	3	4	5	10	15	20	25
Indicator									
Real GDP	7.9	9.3	9.9	10.3	10.7	10.9	10.7	10.5	10.3
Domestic investment	74.5	88.4	88.0	87.1	86.3	75.9	69.0	65.7	65.2
Capital stock	0.0	2.8	5.3	7.5	9.3	14.1	16.0	16.9	17.3
Employment	11.9	12.0	11.2	10.5	9.9	7.6	6.1	5.3	4.7
Real wages	10.3	10.6	10.4	10.3	10.2	9.5	9.1	9.0	9.2
Consumption	–0.6	–0.8	0.2	1.1	1.8	4.3	5.5	5.9	6.0

Source: Americans for Fair Taxation.

Killing Off the "Made in America" Label

If, as business strategists like to say, all business is really war, our own government is guilty of treason against the nation. Calling such competition war may be overstating the case, of course, but the fact remains that we are shooting ourselves in the foot with the income-tax system.

When foreign producers ship products to the United States, most foreign governments do not levy taxes on those products and services sold abroad. The American government, however, exacts business taxes and employment taxes on every American company no matter where its products are sold. In order to stay profitable, American businesses, as stated earlier, commonly embed tax and compliance costs in the price of their goods and services. American businesses pay half of their employees' Social Security and Medicare taxes and are burdened with the second-highest corporate tax rate in the world. Add to these costs the expense of preparing taxes, which amounts to hundreds of billions of dollars a year.

Of course, businesses can jack up their prices to cover the costs of all of these taxes, but doing so reduces their competitive advantage against cheaper foreign goods and services. The only alternative is for them to produce more cheaply, spend less on research and development, or depress the wages of their American workers. Dale Jorgenson, an economist at Harvard, has estimated that our income-tax system causes a 22 percent higher producer cost here in the United States than would exist without the income-tax system. This is killing off the "Made in America" label by creating pressure on employers to move jobs offshore or across our borders in order to better compete.

As the nation struggles to emerge from a terrible recession, unemployment and its human cost continue to grow. It is a painful consequence loop as citizens lose their jobs, can't find new ones, lose their homes, default on debts, and then cause unwilling damage to others in the economy who hold those debts and whose livelihoods are dependent on sales and services in a diminishing pool of discretionary spending. The loss of hope, the loss of opportunities, and the misery that accompanies circumstances largely beyond the control of the individual destroy dreams and change the character and confidence of the nation for the worse.

The fact that our own tax system works against American employment is unforgivable. For the destructive tax system to continue unchanged simply because it produces power and profits for a small number of the political elite at the cost of destroyed dreams and national confidence is beyond unforgivable; it is a betrayal of the public trust and of the nation itself.

How the FairTax Helps the American Automobile Industry

One of the starkest examples of how the FairTax would help American business is the effect it would have on the American automobile industry. The past couple of years have hit these companies hard, but a sweeping change in our tax system could help.

Because the FairTax is levied on the price of consumer goods, at first glance one would think that under this system the price of an automobile would rise significantly. But, upon closer inspection, this is not the case.

Automobiles are generally the second-most-expensive purchase made by an American family (next to a house), and because of all of the embedded taxes in the price of American-made vehicles, this expense is even greater. The United States, in effect, subsidizes foreign-made automobiles by not insisting that tax treatment is equalized with that suffered by American producers on any import that enters our borders. To do so, of course, would be to erect a trade barrier that the Great Depression taught us too well was exactly the wrong way to stimulate needed commerce. The fact is, many foreign governments rebate their domestic companies' taxes (which average eighteen cents on the dollar) on sales and earnings abroad. The United States does not rebate any taxes on products that leave America. The solution for equalizing tax treatment cannot be achieved under the income tax system without the establishment of destructive trade barriers that not only hurt the economy but violate free trade agreements. The solution to equal treatment *is* achieved with an evenly applied tax, not on earnings, but on retail sales within our borders.

Those who argue that the implementation of the FairTax would increase the price of American-made automobiles fail to consider that the cost of the automobile would first *decline* because the hidden taxes would be eliminated. American automakers are quite aware of how competitive their industry is and would be quick to reduce their prices as much as possible if the current tax system was abolished.

While economists do argue over how much producer costs—and therefore the price of the vehicle—will fall, one factor is indisputable: the purchasing power of U.S. consumers will increase. The key question is, How much would an American wage earner have to earn to buy an automobile under the FairTax versus under the income tax? The answer depends on current interest rates and the consumer's own spending under the FairTax, but the following chart suggests good news for consumers. Although interest rates may be lower now than when the research was completed some years ago, whatever the current interest rate, assume a 25 percent reduction.

Consider the following math (shown in the table on the next page). Using a down payment of 10 percent (which is a conservative assumption), and assuming that the buyer pays 7.65 percent payroll taxes and was in the 28 percent marginal tax bracket under the income-tax system, let us see how purchasing a new car becomes more affordable under the FairTax.

ACTUAL COST OF PURCHASING A NEW CAR
(WAGES THAT MUST BE EARNED TO BUY NEW CAR)

Components of new-car cost	Current tax system	FairTax system (25% interest-rate drop)
NADA average vehicle price*	$27,550	$27,550
Down payment of 10%	$2,755	$2,755
Auto loan amount	$24,795	$24,795
Interest rate**	6.79%	5.09%
Interest at above rate for 5 years	$4,545	$3,345
FairTax on new car purchase	—	$8,265
Income tax on interest	$1,273	—
Payroll tax on interest	$348	—
Payroll tax on principal	$2,108	—
Income tax on principal***	$7,714	—
Total taxes	$11,442	$8,265
Total new car including taxes	$43,537	$39,160
Percent difference		**−10.05%**

*NADA average vehicle price 2003.
**Loan rate based on a survey of 32 cities in August 2004.
  Interest rates will drop by 25% under FairTax.
***Assumes purchaser is in the 28% income tax bracket.

Source: Americans for Fair Taxation.

The income tax has stunted the growth of the American economy. The FairTax can help America reach its full potential.

Chapter 3   **The Destructive Income-Tax System**

> "It will be of little avail to the people that the laws are
> made by men of their own choice, if the laws be so
> voluminous that they cannot be read, or so incoherent
> that they cannot be understood . . . or undergo such
> incessant changes that no man who knows what the law
> is today can guess what it will be tomorrow."
>
> —James Madison

F EW AVERAGE PEOPLE can understand the current U.S. tax
code. As April 15 approaches, Americans panic as they
scramble to find receipts, prove deductions, fill out all of the
necessary forms, and make the deadline. Most Americans have
little choice but to pay for tax help. The cost of compliance—
the hours and money spent on preparing tax forms—totaled
close to $300 billion in 2008. It's a confusing mess, and the
amount of taxes actually paid each year commonly comes up
about $350 billion short of what is actually owed by taxpayers.
Some of the shortfall is from cheating, but most is because the
system is so confusing. Any law that requires citizens to spend
hundreds of billions of dollars in order to obey the law is badly
flawed on its face.

The income-tax code itself is a caricature of responsible gov-
ernance. Bloated with favors for individuals and businesses and

so complicated that even the IRS cannot consistently provide sound advice to taxpayers, regulations governing our tax system now take up more than 67,500 pages. Compliance costs are so high that in 2005 Americans spent a little more than twenty-two cents on tax preparation and collection costs for every dollar collected in taxes. We spend more hours on tax forms than the American automobile industry spends making cars—in its best year. That's wasted money and time spent on byzantine complexity created by our own government.

Horror stories abound, and nearly every elected official at the federal level will readily concede that "something has to be done." And yet, despite almost universal condemnation of the income-tax system by both experts and average citizens, little *is* ever done. Proposals to revamp the system to remove the worst examples of corrupting influences are commonly met with derision from Washington, blatant attempts to distort reform proposals, and an unusual bipartisan circling of wagons to protect the corrupt status quo. When an almost universally despised public policy can't be changed by popular demand, the very basis of self-government is put into question.

The tax code invites cheating, but given the complexity of the system, honest mistakes generally cost more than any outright cheating. All told, and after enforcement actions are taken, compliance with the income tax system stands at about 86 percent according to the IRS. And despite angry invective by class-warfare advocates, less than 10 percent of underpayments come from the corporate sector.

This "tax gap," or money owed to the federal government but not paid, inflates the amount owed by average taxpayers by as much as $2,500 a year. The complexity of the system confounds everyone, as the Obama administration discovered when its nominees for cabinet posts and other high-level positions were forced to reveal their own errors.

If we take both former senator Tom Daschle and governor Kathleen Sebelius, two Obama Health and Human Services nominees, and the secretary of the Treasury, Tim Geithner, and even the chairman of the House Ways and Means Committee, Charles Rangel, at face value and assume that they all just made honest errors, the federal taxes owed but not paid by each are really an indictment of the income-tax system itself. It may be hard to accept that the chairman of the House committee that writes tax laws and is staffed with tax lawyers and experts with an almost unlimited budget for research would really not know that he owed income taxes on rental properties he owned. But let's suspend disbelief in his case and give him the benefit of the doubt. Given the complexity of the tax code he oversees, his genuine ignorance is perhaps plausible.

But when the chairman of the House Ways and Means Committee, the man responsible for running the IRS as the secretary of the Treasury, and the nominees to head the agency responsible for Social Security and Medicare say they failed to pay owed taxes because they misunderstood our tax laws, where does that leave the rest of us?

Rangel, Geithner, Sebelius, and Daschle joined the ranks of millions of Americans—and the IRS itself—who are befuddled by the almost indecipherable 67,500 pages of tax rules that accompany the U.S. income-tax system. The amount we spend just to obey—or cheat—our tax laws is about $150 billion more than the total of all the taxpayer stimulus checks mailed out in 2008.

Our tax system has become an expensive and confusing collection of thousands of political favors, ambiguous rules that invite all manner of tax avoidance strategies and ill-considered congressional attempts to manipulate citizen behavior. Nearly a century of government appetite for more and more taxpayer wealth and often ham-handed tinkering has transformed what began as a relatively simple tax on the rich into a multiheaded monster that confounds even the smartest among us.

How We Came to Adopt Direct Taxation—The Income Tax

"What is the difference between a taxidermist and a tax collector? The taxidermist takes only your skin." — MARK TWAIN

Our current income-tax system began as political brinksman-ship in Congress. It was a "double dare" to Republicans by House Democrats in 1912 to vote against legislation that, for the first time, took taxes from the earnings of the rich. With the emergence of the fabulously wealthy owners and shareholders of railroads, newspapers, and steel, coal, and oil companies, the country was ripe for class warfare. Teddy Roosevelt, a leader in the "progressive" wing of the Republican Party, favored the new income tax, which would "soak the rich" and, supposedly, benefit the poor.

The whole idea of an income tax had been debated for years. The first working income tax actually passed Congress during the Civil War. Although collection was problematic, in 1861 Congress did enact an income tax of 3 percent on earnings be-tween $600 and $10,000 a year. Earnings over $10,000 a year (about $170,000 in today's dollars) were subject to a tax of 5 percent. Mark Twain may have been inspired to quip about taxes after unwittingly bragging for some hours to an interested stranger about his wealth—only to discover that the fellow was, in fact, a tax assessor tasked with ferreting out such wealth on behalf of the federal government. Too late to save Twain a hefty tax bill, these early income taxes were repealed by 1872. A later version was enacted in 1894 without a constitutional amendment and was rejected by the Supreme Court as unconstitutional in 1895.

The issue had received national attention, of course, and was seen by many in the public as a way to make the rich pay their fair share. But after the Supreme Court's reasoning that an income tax violated the Constitution's prohibition against direct taxation (article 1, section 9), many outside Washington felt the issue dead forever.

But the political class in Washington was hungry to expand the role of the federal government by taking on more authority and power than state and local governments. Scores of income-tax bills were filed and defeated over the next two decades by members of Congress determined to reverse the balance of power between the federal government and the "lower" levels of government. The original concept of the framers of the Constitution, after all, was a small role for the federal government and a much more significant role for local and state governments, where the citizen's voice was more pronounced and ever present.

But there was a huge difference of opinion between Democrats and Republicans on the issue, and the income tax was a strong and popular plank in the Democrats' national platforms of 1896 and 1908. The debate raged between those who opposed any income tax and those who promised to tax the rich so that others, less successful in our growing economy, might enjoy some of the fruits of others' labors. It was an argument for the pure redistribution of wealth based on the "promise" that only the filthy rich would ever pay.

Texas senator Joseph Weldon Bailey, a Democrat, finally set into motion enactment of the modern-day income tax, even though he was personally opposed to such an idea. By most accounts, he introduced the measure in the Senate merely as a tactic to embarrass Republicans as defenders of the rich. Instead of risking such embarrassment, and because the liberal wing of the Republican Party supported such a tax, House and Senate Republicans agreed to pass such a bill only if the new tax was contingent upon the states' approval of a constitutional amendment—which they felt was certain to fail. The measure passed unanimously in the Senate and with only token resistance in the House.

With promises to the public that such a tax would only affect the rich, the amendment was ratified on February 12, 1913. At first, these promises proved true, with less than 1 percent of the public paying any income tax. Today, once again, fewer and fewer Americans pay income taxes. More and more of the ever-greater federal revenues are paid by those Americans who are most successful—and, because of the national debt, by future generations of Americans. One might argue that the federal debts in the trillions of dollars that are now secured by the future earnings of unborn Americans return us to a system of "taxation without representation."

Interestingly, Senator Bailey suffered an irony of history—or perhaps political retribution—when he was forced to resign in 1911, not because he was the "father of the income tax" or the champion of redistribution of wealth but because his ties to and profits from Standard Oil—a hated symbol of class differences—were revealed in a nasty public fight with another senator.

In the years since, the income tax has come to pervade every aspect of American life. There was a time, now forgotten, when few Americans believed it was anyone's business how much a family earned, how much they spent, or what they spent money on. Today, the most personal details of life revealed in our financial records are, by law, open to the scrutiny of government officials and sometimes, as during the Nixon years, the basis of political harassment. Today there is no question that the Founding Fathers' original design of strong local and state governments has been eclipsed by the power of the federal government collecting and spending huge amounts of income taxes.

The income-tax code has grown over the years like the infamous kudzu vine. Almost one hundred years of congressional amendments to the tax code, court decisions, and taxpayer/IRS disputes have swelled the tax code to more than 2.1 million words. Despite every promise to simplify the system, it only gets more complicated because so many tax breaks, gimmicks, and loopholes are granted in every session of Congress and because almost every "special circumstance" requires more sections, more definitions, and more complexity.

Rather than merely serving as an efficient mechanism to collect revenues for our collective needs, the system has become an end unto itself, supporting a multibillion-dollar annual lobbying industry. According to one recent study by three University of Kansas tax law professors, corporations saw a reduction of more than $220 in owed taxes for every dollar spent on lobbying. With a single tax break in 2004, five hundred American companies earned a 22,000 percent rate of return on their lobbying "investment."

Considering that the lobbying examined in this single study saved the companies more than $100 billion in taxes, there is no reason that such lobbying won't continue to win breaks for a few and further complicate the system for all. One of the authors of the study, Stephen W. Mazza, was quoted in the *Washington Post*, saying, "There's always been speculation that lobbying is a lucrative area. We've been able to come up with quantifiable returns and show that it really is the case." Lucrative, indeed. In just one example from the study, drugmaker Eli Lilly and Company reported spending $8.52 million in lobbying and saving $2 billion in taxes.

As tax lawyer and financial blogger Hale Stewart writes, "There are a ton of special interest giveaways in the tax code. . . . At least half of the items in sections 101–140 (items specifically excluded from gross income) are there for a particular special interest. Ever wonder why life insurance isn't included in the recipient's gross income? Ask the insurance industry."

Such lobbying clout is not, of course, available to the average American. While some provisions do benefit the ordinary taxpayer, many more are aimed at the favored few with money and lobbying clout. Taxpayers now pay income taxes in brackets ranging from 15 percent to 39.6 percent depending on income. Payroll taxes are added on top of income taxes and withheld from paychecks (as are income taxes). When taken together, for all but the poorest Americans, our true federal tax rates range from 30.3 percent to 43.3 percent. In 2001 the average taxpayer paid more than $8,000 in annual income taxes. But if everyone who owed taxes actually paid all the taxes due, the average taxpayer would owe $2,640 less, a reduction of more than 32 percent. As Congressman John Linder, the sponsor of FairTax legislation, likes to say, "Would you rather pay 23 percent (at most) of what you spend or an average of 30 percent of what you earn?"

And then there is the work we must do to obey the law. In 1955 the income-tax code amounted to a little over 400,000 words; today it is more than 2.1 million words. The code has become so complicated that it invites both cheating and mistakes. According to the IRS itself, if tax compliance were an industry, it would be one of the largest in the United States, consuming 7.6 billion hours of Americans' time annually. That amount of work hours, by the way, requires the equivalent of 3.8 million full-time workers.

The simplicity of the FairTax stands in stark contrast to the complexity of the income-tax system. Obeying national tax laws will no longer be a matter of expert interpretation of ambiguous definitions. Today, even the IRS cannot guarantee the advice it provides to taxpayers. Some studies have shown that nearly half of all such advice is wrong. It's really the fault not of the IRS but of the system created by Congress. The income-tax system has become so complex because the terms defining the tax system have been tortured into indecipherability by the profit and political motives of those on congressional tax-writing committees.

Because taxes are paid at the cash register under the FairTax and remitted to the existing state sales-tax collection system, the IRS will no longer be needed to collect federal taxes. The savings achieved by shuttering the IRS will amount to billions of dollars annually, but these savings will be dwarfed by the saved costs—and headaches—of preparing individual tax filings.

Abolition of the IRS does not mean that federal enforcement of our tax system will end but that the Treasury Department instead of the IRS will look at the relatively simple ratio between retail sales made and taxes remitted. In addition, compliance oversight by federal authorities will extend over a far smaller universe of retail outlets rather than the one currently overseen by the IRS, which is tasked with ensuring compliance for both businesses and individual taxpayers. The herculean responsibility of oversight and enforcement of more than 120 million individual taxpayers' returns is eliminated with the Fair-Tax. On the citizens' side of the tax equation, the headaches of

April 15 are abolished and replaced with the more enjoyable activities of a typical spring day.

Those who have made much of the promise to end the IRS under the FairTax are sometimes subject to charges of misleading the public about the need for continued compliance costs and enforcement. This is because some critics have raised the concern that without strict enforcement and oversight a high sales tax will create a robust off-the-books economy and that such an approach will be plagued by wholesale attempts to cheat the system. The critics are both right and wrong.

While it is true that no federal tax system can exist without attempts at cheating, and the FairTax will present its own unique cheating temptations, there are good reasons why the FairTax compliance rate will be better than that of the income tax. FairTax advocates and independent economists remind critics that more than 80 percent of retail sales today come from a relatively few superretailers like Wal-Mart. It is unlikely that such superchains will risk everything by cheating. Additionally, the universe for compliance oversight by the federal government will be far smaller, with 120 million individual returns eliminated under the FairTax. And under the income tax system it takes only one person to cheat—the filer. Under the Fair-Tax, it takes two to cheat—the retailer and the consumer.

Perfection can be found in church or in the smile of a child, perhaps, but not in any national tax system. The real way to judge the FairTax is not by the problems that will inevitably be encountered in the administration of the system—because they *will* exist—but by a qualitative comparison between the advantages and disadvantages of each system when taken as a whole. Lacking the more than 67,500 pages of definitions and rules of the income-tax code, the FairTax is relatively simple and straight-forward. For individual taxpayers, there are no compliance costs.

For businesses collecting and paying the tax there is one question: did you collect and remit 23 percent of the total retail sales amount?

A Case in Point—Tax Committee Dysfunction Exposed

As I've written, under the income-tax code debt is more favorable than wealth, married people pay more than singles, and business decisions are commonly made on the basis of tax consequences instead of sound practices and growth. The Alternative Minimum Tax, once designed to squeeze taxes from a few hundred very wealthy people who had figured out how to legally underpay millions of dollars, now threatens to add more than $2,000 a year to the tax bills of twenty million middle-class Americans because of an error in the way the law was originally written and because the government now counts on that revenue.

The Alternative Minimum Tax is only the most recent reminder of the fact that the congressional tax-writing process is badly broken and that our entirely political system of writing tax laws renders Congress incapable of correcting even the most obvious assaults on the well-being of American taxpayers.

The Alternative Minimum Tax was created in 1969 to capture taxes from 155 families who were so rich and so skilled at using the many arcane provisions of the tax code that they paid little or no income taxes. But because Congress erred and failed to index the provision for inflation, as many as twenty-three to twenty-five million middle-class taxpayers have already lost eligibility for deductions for children, real estate, and state taxes, as well as other exemptions and deductions. Oops!

Okay, so the humans in Congress made a human error and

then rushed to correct it—right? Wrong. Because of the dishonesty in the budget-writing process in Congress, the federal government has grown dependent on the projected income from the Alternative Minimum Tax in order to offset existing debt on the books and continued spending. The government now counts on $800 billion to $1.5 trillion over the next decade in taxes from people who were never intended to be taxed so that an equal amount of spending and debt can be hidden. Rather than change this dishonest accounting, Congress has simply legislated "patches" that temporarily "erase" this provision of the tax code one year at a time.

Now that our borrowing, spending, and ambitious programs to repair health care, education, and the environment have combined with trillions of dollars of government bailout and economic-stimulus spending programs, the political and moral barriers holding back application of this unintended tax have almost dissolved. Washington, in its hunger for more and more taxpayer earnings, will almost certainly put fingers to ears and squeeze eyes shut to this obvious error and assault on reason.

With at least $75,000 a year in income, taxpayers in high-cost areas of the nation like New York City and most other major urban areas will learn that they are considered by Congress to be "wealthy" and subject to the AMT. In 2005, the Tax Policy Center and the Treasury Department estimated that around 15 percent of households with incomes between $75,000 and $100,000 must pay the AMT, up from only 2 percent to 3 percent in 2000, with the percentage increasing at higher incomes. Because the tax is not indexed to inflation, the percentage of affected Americans will continue to grow. As it now stands, these taxpayers will suffer both insult and injury because when the existing tax law is implemented, penalties will be assessed on millions of unsuspecting citizens for underwith-holding sufficient taxes under the AMT.

There are few more stark examples of public policy hurting the public than the AMT and the income-tax system. Even gross errors like the AMT cannot, once legislated, be easily reversed. The double calculations required to assess tax liability under the AMT wrongly double the cost of tax compliance, at the very least. According to the IRS's taxpayer advocate, determining whether someone owes the AMT can require reading nine pages of instructions and completing a sixteen-line work sheet and a fifty-five-line form.

TAXES CAUSE ENOUGH headaches as it is, even without the endless amount of time, energy, and money spent to prepare them. The FairTax may not be perfect, but it's a lot less painful.

Chapter 4 **Restoring the Relationship Between Citizen and Government**

"The difference between death and taxes is death doesn't get worse every time Congress meets."

—Will Rogers

Without an easily understood linkage between our paychecks and government spending, our own majority-rule democracy—actually a constitutional republic, of course—is subject to irresponsible appeals by cynical candidates and officeholders to spend our common wealth. They have learned, too well, that votes can be bought with what seems like "free money" to many voters. That money really comes out of our paychecks, our hard work, and our job-creating investments. Payroll withholding and payroll taxes, however, hide that reality from view, and constant class-warfare tactics by political operatives and candidates for office obscure the truth that taxes always get paid, one way or another, by consumers and workers.

Most Americans balance their monthly budgets; those who don't lose their creditworthiness. Not so with government. The destructive foolishness of spending so much more than we collect in taxes is only possible because of accepted dishonesty by both parties in the federal budgeting process and, significantly, because the cost of what is spent by our government is hidden from view. Payroll withholding of taxes was originally conceived by the famed Nobel Prize–winning economist Milton Friedman—though even he later admitted regretting it.

Withholding taxes from paychecks ensures that too few citizens realize the full impact of government promises on their own financial health. This element of our tax collection system makes it very difficult for the voting populace to give "informed consent" and actually undermines majority rule in our form of democracy.

It is not at all uncommon to hear a cheery exclamation that the worker "paid nothing" but got money *back* from the federal government after April 15. It is a sleight of hand of epic proportions and one that makes government spending well beyond our means seem downright attractive. It is a dangerous illusion, however, that threatens the very foundation of our economy.

To understand the advantages of the FairTax, one must also understand the real inherent dangers of our income-tax system. Our tax system works against the nation in two profoundly destructive and significant ways. First, as already mentioned, it taxes and weakens the very things that make our economy strong. Second, our tax system makes it too easy for politicians to buy American votes with money that does not on the surface seem to be coming out of citizens' paychecks. The first has slowed our economy by retarding job creation and investment, while the second has enabled—and even popularized—a path of unsustainable federal spending and debt that exposes what may very well prove to be the Achilles' heel of our democracy.

Under the FairTax, a citizen's earnings belong first to the

citizen, unlike under the income tax, which assumes that a citizen's earnings belong first to the government, with the remainder being available for our individual "pursuit of happiness." This is no small distinction. Indeed, one might conclude that when a worker is only taking home what is left over after government takes its share, we have become the very definition of modern-day "serfs." Not quite what our Founding Fathers had in mind.

By contrast, individuals control how much tax they pay under the FairTax. Because federal taxes under the FairTax plan are paid upon consumption and because each purchase receipt includes the cost of the federal tax, the cost of the federal government finally becomes clear to every consumer. New transparency that connects taxes with earnings will likely lead to new consumer/taxpayer pressure on elected officials to restrain government spending of what will finally be clearly seen as our own wealth.

The most compelling virtue of the FairTax may very well be that it turns every consumer in the United States into a concerned taxpaying stakeholder. The FairTax makes it possible for the majority to have a real say in our nation's fiscal decisions by disclosing the cost of those decisions to every consumer. What is the cost of new spending (out of my pocket) and what is the benefit? That becomes the new question on the lips of every taxpayer/consumer. A thoughtful and persuasive explanation of why new spending is justified becomes a political necessity for government officials. In truth, it should have always been this way. Because the FairTax makes government spending so transparent in terms of what comes out of our dollars, government spending and the earnings of citizens can no longer be easily divorced.

Let's consider for a moment how that might affect an imaginary legislative proposal.

Say, for example, our leaders decide that colonization of the moon requires increasing the FairTax rate from the proposed 23 percent to 25 percent on all purchases. Every consumer will almost certainly have something to say about that. Is that a good investment coming out of every consumer dollar spent? It's a fair and necessary question that is hardly ever asked at present. Today, by contrast, massive spending for entitlements, stimulus projects, pet projects, "earmarks," and every other government program seems like "free money" to a lot of voters because such spending has become so seemingly divorced from our earnings.

The effect is destructive, as politicians from both parties have taken us down a path of unsustainable spending. Some economists, like Larry Kotlikoff of Boston University, view current and obligated future structural government debt at the local, state, and federal levels as so large that it threatens the "full faith and credit" of the United States. Others wonder if we are approaching the point where foreign creditors no longer believe that we can ever satisfy such debt—the definition of bankruptcy.

Our collective and self-defeating answer to such worries has been to spend more—both to assuage public fears and to address real needs. As I have mentioned, we are now spending the earnings of our children and grandchildren on both the challenges of a modern society and the politically popular wishes of entrenched interest groups across the political spectrum. The question of how to raise more taxpayer money so government can do more—or give away more—is, of course, the subject of bitter and partisan debate that has almost come to define the difference between conservatives and liberals, although both sides have their "favorites" for spending of collective wealth and almost all are guilty of "earmarking" appropriations for home-town consumption.

From the Right, the most popular answer has been to collect less by legislating tax cuts, in the legitimate hope that such cuts will stimulate the economy, which will, in turn, produce more tax revenues. The Left generally argues that we should collect more taxes from big businesses and the wealthy (which, as I've already explained at length, is not as simple as it seems) and put more dollars into programs that help all or some Americans. If we were not already in such deep debt, the debate between the two sides might make sense and a rational middle ground might be achieved. But with more than $12 trillion of national debt and another $40–60 trillion of debt at the state and local level, this endless argument begins to look a lot like clueless ideologues standing in the middle of a long, parched desert, locked in an endless argument over whether to bake bread or grow wheat. By all rights, the American people should decide the argument, but it is almost impossible for us to make an informed decision given the common perception that such spending has little to do with our own wealth and given the hiding of what new spending and borrowing does to the true size of the national debt.

There is another very powerful reason that politicians love divorcing the perception of government spending from our earnings. Simply put, those in charge of such spending become more powerful and usually more popular with voters through the promises they make. Cloaked by ideological arguments and passions, much of the underlying motivation for such growth comes down to the entirely human love of power and the desire to be reelected.

This "outsider's" perspective is, of course, heresy to all those who work to pit us against one another in every election and represents yet another reason the FairTax is less than welcome in Washington. If you fear that this line of reasoning is building toward a partisan attack on either party, you should both relax and be afraid, because the reality is even worse than you think. The corruption of both the tax system and the appropriations process that hides our real debt is entirely bipartisan. Both parties have betrayed the majority rule of the people by obscuring the truth about the cost of government. It's human, not ideological, and it hurts every American.

Behind the destructive tax system that undergirds much of the class debate about how government can get more of our money is a single figure that, as just one more example, reveals a lot about the charade of fiscal responsibility on the part of our government. In 2007 the nation borrowed about $160 billion from foreign lenders to send stimulus checks to taxpayers to spark consumption at home. In the months leading up to April 15 of that same year, paradoxically, Americans spent an estimated $300 billion on tax preparation costs. In other words, we wasted almost twice as much money on tax complexity created by our own government as we borrowed and distributed to stimulate our economy. The FairTax eliminates those costs, spurs investment, and makes clear what government promises cost each American. In this the FairTax may prove to be not just a better national tax system but the best way to save both our economy and informed majority rule in our democracy.

Chapter 5   **How the Government Grows**

> "I hope a tax will be preferred [to a loan that threatens to saddle us with a perpetual debt], because it will awaken the attention of the people and make reformation and economy the principle of the next election. The frequent recurrence of this chastening operation can alone restrain the propensity of governments to enlarge expense beyond income."
>
> —Thomas Jefferson to Albert Gallatin, 1820

T HE GROWTH OF the federal government, once much smaller than state and local governments, is a direct consequence of the income tax. Many would argue this is a healthy development, since programs like Social Security and Medicare would not be possible without such growth. It's true that a modern society requires an evolved form of government to address the common good and protect individual liberties. In truth, however, we have traded some of that individual liberty for greater security. As long as such trade-offs are within the protections of our Constitution and as long as they are approved by the majority will of an informed populace, such an evolution is the right of the citizenry and properly remains within the control of the body politic.

But there are a lot of obvious examples that prove that "informed consent" by the people has been severely undermined by accounting gimmicks, PR spin, unhealthy citizen dependence on government programs (which skews perspective), and indecipherable complexity. Let's look at one huge example of government spin that hides the true obligations of the public to foreign creditors now and in the future: the national debt.

Most government officials—including our Treasury secretary—would tell you that the national debt now hovers around a shocking $12 trillion. That's scary enough, but it's actually worse. Interest payments on the debt alone cost $452 billion last year—the largest federal spending category after Medicare/Medicaid, Social Security, and defense. But even this fails to tell the whole story.

The Peter G. Peterson Foundation, established by a former commerce secretary to address fiscal sustainability issues, argues that the $11.4 trillion debt figure fails to account for roughly $45 trillion in unlisted liabilities and unfunded retirement and health-care commitments. The federal government uses cash accounting rather than accrual accounting to arrive at its figures. This hides huge amounts of borrowed money. Until payments are due, the debt is not reflected in reports on the actual state of our true fiscal health—or, put another way, what each of us owes.

Writing in the *Nebraska Law Review* in 2003, George Washington University law professor Cheryl Block said that such accounting tricks are the same ones used by corporations prosecuted for massive frauds upon stockholders and the public. Congress "has been guilty of using accounting devices remarkably similar to those used by Enron, WorldCom and others to 'cook the books' and to mislead the public with regard to government finances," she wrote.

Social Security and Medicare face an unfunded liability of $33.2 trillion, an off-the-books figure far greater than the currently understood national debt. Spending categories that include propping up banks, appropriations for emergencies, and many other categories of real spending, secured by increasing debt, also end up "off budget." And yet despite this frightening amount of debt, Congress still found $200 million to spend on three high-end private jets to whisk members around the country and world. Where did this money come from? Well, our government borrowed it, of course, against our future earnings. Stories like this make us wonder, Do we really have a say in how our leaders spend our money, and in the process gamble on our futures?

Our Social Security program only pretends to divorce retirement security from the birthrate. It's a Ponzi scheme of the first order that has been routinely raided for other government spending. In truth, from caveman days to the present, retirement security has been an intergenerational formula: have a lot of kids if you want to rest easier in your old age. That has not changed under Social Security, but FICA taxes provide the federal government with trillions of dollars to mask other spending and debt. That practice, however, means an ever-closer day of reckoning as the trillions of dollars in tax money already collected for baby-boomer retirement must be paid out. So where's the money? In Treasury notes that are secured by—you guessed it—the earnings of the next generations.

When the birthrate drops, costs to the next generations of programs like Social Security and Medicare go up—perhaps unsustainably, since the government owes the same amount but there are fewer people to pay it. Once such programs are enacted, it has proven almost impossible to adjust them to new realities like falling birthrates or even to slow their growth, because of the irresistible attraction of candidates and officeholders to buying votes with increased spending and because of the understandable fear that such an idea produces in a population that has come to depend on government promises and programs. The reality of financial ruin, however, has not stopped politicians and would-be politicians from using these programs to buy votes by promising more spending. In a sense, it is a political straitjacket that cannot be shed if one wants to be elected and reelected—so, too many reason, why not run with it?

Our political system is so awash in money and both the seeking and peddling of influence that spending and taxing decisions based on political gain—whether they involve subsidies or tax breaks—are more the rule than the exception. The benefits of spending are so much more pronounced than the more substantial, though less immediate, benefits of restraint that few politicians can resist irresponsible actions that lead to greater and greater debt. In other words, our dollars are often spent less on the common good than on the private interests of those who wield influence in Washington, D.C.

The danger for the nation is that spending on federal programs has outpaced the amount of money available to fund these programs. Because increases in spending for "entitlements" are population and formula driven, reining in such spending has proven politically impossible and terrifying to those who have come to depend on such benefits. We have created a society that is increasingly dependent on money collected from the public and then redistributed to the public through cash payments, programs, and tax breaks. Such a system fundamentally changes the relationship between citizen and government, is inherently resistant to limits on spending, and is prone to even more special-interest pressure to increase spending. It's a one-way street to eventual collapse only delayed by more government accounting gimmicks that cover up and push to the future the real consequences of debt, hidden taxes, and ever-larger borrowing from foreign creditors.

Even a conservative president like George W. Bush succumbed to political operatives' whispering that a new senior-citizen prescription-drug benefit—which would cost tens of billions of dollars and be all but uncontainable—would win him the votes he needed for his second term. They were right. Out-of-control earmarks that "bring the bacon home" to local voters, such as the all-but-unused John Murtha airport or the "bridge to nowhere" in Alaska, provide more prime examples of votes bought with the borrowed national treasury—and now the earnings of coming generations. For a nation founded on outrage over "no taxation without representation," our government—and indeed, the American voter—treats the tax burdens we are imposing on future generations with an amazingly cavalier attitude.

Dangerously, when taxpayer revenues are not sufficient to sustain spending (or the political ambitions of officeholders) we have simply—and wrongly—borrowed more and more from foreign lenders, pledging the earnings of our citizens, their children, and their grandchildren to secure the growing debt. Today even some third-world countries hold quantities of American debt that, if sold in a block at a loss, would threaten the very foundation of our economy, not to mention the well-being of the American taxpayer.

More than two hundred years ago Scottish historian and professor Alexander Fraser Tytler is said to have written, "a democracy cannot exist as a permanent form of government. It can only exist until the voters discover that they can vote themselves largesse from the public treasury. From that moment on, the majority always votes for the candidates promising the most benefits from the public treasury with the result that a democracy always collapses over loose fiscal policy, always followed by a dictatorship. The average age of the world's greatest civilizations has been 200 years." There is some disagreement whether Tytler, in fact, wrote these words but the meaning is nonetheless relevant today.

With the national debt now totaling more than $12 trillion—and growing fast with the latest recovery and stimulus programs—it is fair to ask, Is this theory proving true here in the United States?

Today the top 1 percent of income earners pays 39.9 percent of all federal taxes while the bottom half of the earning population pays just over 3 percent. More than a third of the nation's citizens pay no income taxes at all. Of course, when politicians seek votes, they try to woo the majority, not the minority, so it is no wonder that politicians have become the enthusiastic agents of Tytler's prediction.

One need only look at the last several national elections to realize that promises of prescription drug benefits for seniors, universal health care for all, new roads and new schools, and other promises to various constituencies and income groups are really promises of spending that, even if the spending is needed, buy votes. All of these programs cost money. Where does this money come from? Straight out of the taxpayer's pocket.

This is not new. Almost since the founding of the nation, our government has voted subsidies for sugar growers, price supports for various other commodities, and special benefits to politically important individuals and industries and groups that hold significant influence. Many programs seem worthy; others seem to represent nothing more than the cynical calculations of political operatives, issue advocates, and policy experts who come together to calculate how to trade payoffs for votes.

The problem with buying votes in this manner is that the wealth that pays for these programs and policies is our own, and such spending has put us on an unsustainable path of ever-deepening debt. When the debt becomes so great that the taxes necessary to satisfy creditors take away the motivation of workers to produce, to invent, and to move up to the next economic level of success, the entire system begins to unwind, becoming less and less "profitable" to government.

Money spent on taxes and tax-avoidance strategies leaves less money available for job creation, research, and growth. Lower productivity means less wealth is produced, and a point is reached when no reasonable person or institution any longer believes the debt can be satisfied. No one knows the exact national debt figure that will finally blow a hole in foreign and domestic investors' confidence in our creditworthiness, but some economists have sounded dire warnings that we are quickly approaching that number.

Congressional tax-writing committees like the House Ways and Means Committee, the Joint Committee on Taxation, and the Senate Finance Committee (and the subcommittees of each) get the first bite of the political favoritism apple by reducing the taxes owed by various favored individuals, constituencies, and industries. Sometimes, although it's often ignored, a particular tax break granted applies only to a single individual or local business. More often, powerful industries are able to marshal the political clout—and cold cash—necessary to win favored treatment.

Our Founding Fathers called a tax on labor "direct taxation" and believed it a dangerously slippery slope that, along with unpaid national debts, would eventually lead to economic ruin. Before it was amended, the Constitution banned such a tax. Thomas Jefferson even wrote that the national government should take on no debt that could not be repaid within nineteen years, so that federal debt could not be passed on to future generations. The Founding Fathers also reasoned that taxing the fruits of citizens' labor worked against the principle of individual liberty so important in creating our form of government.

As I said above, more than a third of Americans pay no income tax at all. Low-income couples who pay no income tax actually get money back from the federal government through the Earned Income Tax Credit. These reimbursements offset taxes paid by the poor to Social Security and Medicare through FICA payroll taxes. President Obama has suggested expanding this program. Under the president's plan, the number of citizens who pay no income tax will rise to more than 40 percent.

On the other hand, the top 1 percent of earners in the United States pay 39.9 percent of income taxes, according to the IRS. The top quarter of earners pay 86.3 percent. That means that those earning more than $64,702 pay almost 90 percent of income taxes. It also means that the top 1 percent of earners pay about the same combined amount of income taxes as the bottom 95 percent of Americans.

But there are holes in this too-simple picture. The IRS figures used in these calculations only consider income taxes paid and don't include FICA payroll taxes. Payroll taxes for Social Security and Medicare amount to 15.3 percent of wages for those who earn up to $97,500 a year. Above that income level, the Social Security tax is not collected and the Medicare tax continues at a rate of 2.6 percent. Most Americans pay more toward Social Security and Medicare than they pay in income taxes.

Employers pay half of the FICA tax, and employees pay the other half. The self-employed pay the full rate of 15.3 percent on earnings up to $102,500 a year and pay the full Medicare tax on earnings above that figure. According to the Tax Policy Center, when we add payroll taxes into the calculation, the top 20 percent of Americans pay 72 percent of the combined total of income and payroll taxes, and the bottom 20 percent pay less than 0.5 percent. And considering both taxes, the top 1 percent of Americans pay 27.5 percent of the total taxes collected.

Those contrasts may become even more pronounced if tax proposals by the Obama administration find footing in Congress. The Bush-era tax cuts will expire, raising the tax rate on the highest income bracket to almost 40 percent. If enacted, national health-care reform must be paid for or a new trillion-dollar debt gets added to taxpayers' bills. Capital gains taxes, the tax paid to the government on the growth of private investments, will almost certainly go up with campaign-trail-suggested cuts delayed until at least 2014. Energy companies will pass along their higher taxes to consumers for gasoline, home heating oil, natural gas, and electricity if campaign promises to improve the environment with a "carbon tax" come true. Food prices, dependent on energy costs, will also spike, as they did when Congress decided to give tax breaks to corn growers who sold their crops to ethanol producers.

Many of the new proposed taxes will be borne across the economic spectrum as food, energy, and health-care expenses go up. Others, such as increases in capital gains taxes and marginal rates, will put a heavier burden on the "investor" class that typically risks the greatest amounts of private capital on growth.

Higher-income earners, by definition, have more wealth. Top earners' relative share of wealth has increased in recent years, as has their share of taxes paid. The real question for the nation is how much can be taken from those who work or who are the most successful in order to distribute that wealth to those who don't work or who are not as successful.

I'll leave it to economists to debate this question using tax rates, productivity, investment in the economy, charitable contribution rates under different tax levels, and so on. The general argument, however, is over the contention that the lower the tax rate on upper-income earners, the more the economy grows, because this is the segment of the population that invests most. Those who disagree argue that the wealthy should pay more so the government can provide social services, benefits, and opportunities for upward mobility to those with less.

Each view may have merit in healthy economic times. I would argue, on the other hand, that neither side is right when the overall national debt is so high that it becomes an unbearable weight on everyone. But this central argument and the hundreds of "proofs" brought forward by each side consume the political process and convince few outside the already-convinced "choir" the opponents are preaching to.

In this, American politicians make class warfare a staple of domestic politics. When Americans are pitted against one another, the passions of citizens are fanned for the political benefit of candidates on either side of the divide created by—you guessed it—our politicians. It's a destructive and self-serving game that obscures the fact that we are, in truth, entirely interdependent. Everything changes with the FairTax because it takes the penalties off productivity and expansion of the economy. That translates into more personal wealth—and yes, more tax revenues for government.

The FairTax expands the tax base and delivers relief to all taxpayers, who are, after all, riding in the same economic boat. The poor are the single greatest beneficiaries of a new system of taxation that eliminates highly regressive FICA taxes. The middle class sees the second-largest chunk of tax relief. The "wealthy," a changing definition out of Washington, find that investment income is no longer taxed. Every segment benefits from the lifting of the weight of taxation from capital formation, savings, and work. And all Americans benefit from dramatically increased investment in the American economy when the United States becomes the "offshore tax haven" to the world.

Chapter 6   Who Wins Under the FairTax?

> "All duties upon articles of consumption, may be compared to a fluid, which will, in time, find its level with the means of paying them. The amount to be contributed by each citizen will in a degree be at his own option, and can be regulated by an attention to his resources. The rich may be extravagant, the poor can be frugal. . . . It is a signal advantage of taxes on articles of consumption, that they contain in their own nature a security against excess."
>
> —Alexander Hamilton

U NDER THE INCOME-TAX system someone has to lose for someone else to win. Politicians have become very skilled at pitting income groups against one another in our tax debates. We've all seen it and can recognize this game, which is politically profitable for candidates and interest groups. The FairTax changes the terms of the debate from who wins and who loses to whether we all—or at least most of us—agree that government spending on particular programs is justified.

Under the FairTax, *almost* everyone wins because the tax base itself is greatly expanded. When more people pay into the system, the burden on almost all individuals is reduced. Because of this fact, class warfare among income groups disappears as a weapon in the national tax system. Jealousy and envy may be part of human nature, but the FairTax cannot be exploited by elected officials and candidates in tax debates that pit Americans against one another.

The "losers" under the FairTax are foreign producers who have an advantage in our markets, illegal immigrants who now pay no income taxes, and all those who have operated under the table to avoid notice under the income-tax system. Tax lobbyists are big losers under the FairTax because there are no opportunities to game the legislative system for profit. The entire industry that has grown up around the tax-writing committees in Washington also loses, although I would argue that, as Americans, its participants equally win with recovery of the American economy.

Despite the class-warfare arguments and destructive consequences of the current tax system, pooling some of our money to cover the costs of things that benefit us seems like a pretty good idea. We may disagree about what to spend the money on, about how much should be taken from citizens, and about how much government can practically deliver, but societal needs simply can't be met without contributions from all.

Most would agree that we have legitimate needs for government revenue to provide for the common good. Although almost every argument for shifting taxes, whether from the Right or from the Left, is expressed in these terms, the ideological arguments are too often just cynical camouflage designed to inflame the passions of voters in order to win votes. There is no tax burden shifting under the FairTax, but changes will, by definition and by deliberate design, have to win agreement from the entire American population of consumers, because the FairTax is levied on all.

Okay, we know we only get back a fraction of the value of each tax dollar we contribute, because of retirement-plan nest feathering in the Pentagon, Department of Veterans Affairs employees who don't show up to work, and lax controls on government credit cards, to name just three reasons. Unfortunately, after all the promises over the years to eliminate waste, it seems there is only so much that operationally distant legislators or even the president can do to get more value for our money. Such waste and even outright fraud doesn't change the fact that we need the magnitudes of scale that government agencies bring to the challenges of a modern society.

Defense of the nation, a functioning and safe highway system, the ability to respond to emergencies, a safe food supply, drugs that work, a weather warning system, an effective criminal justice system, a diplomatic system, and a safety net for the poor are just a few things that have gradually been accepted by the public as legitimate and necessary uses of our pooled resources at the state, local, or federal levels. The arguments about how to allocate our shared resources will, of course, continue even if the FairTax is enacted, but the main issue becomes less a matter of who should pay more or pay less and more a matter of whether politicians can win public consensus about the importance of all of us paying part of our wealth for needed government activities. It's a straightforward cost-benefit argument. That's a far healthier, not to mention more honest, relationship between citizens and their government.

The American Poor

The poor benefit most from the FairTax because of the elimination of FICA taxes and the embedded tax costs in retail prices, as well as the monthly prebate that covers the cost of the necessities of life. Growth in job creation, investment, and savings spurred by the FairTax will also help those who still strive so hard to achieve the American dream. With trillions of dollars coming into our economy from offshore and American investment freed from government-created tax hobbles, American employers will be hungry for new employees. This means better wages, better benefits, and more jobs to choose from.

You may be wondering how the FairTax actually helps the poor, because under our current tax system, poor and low-income Americans don't pay income taxes—at least not directly. In fact, about 42 percent of Americans don't pay any income taxes (more about that later). But every American, no matter his or her income level, does pay FICA taxes. From the first dollar earned, whether you earn $8 an hour or $1,000 an hour, 7.65 percent is paid to the federal government for Social Security and Medicare. This amount is doubled to 15.3 percent for the self-employed. This highly regressive flat tax, whose proceeds have been spent by our government on other pursuits instead of saved for our futures, is eliminated under the FairTax.

In fact, Professor Kotlikoff of Boston University argues that those who receive the Earned Income Tax Credit suffer the perverse effect of punitively high marginal tax rates. He writes, "For some low- and middle-income households, the marginal tax on working under our current tax system is more than twice the 23 percent FairTax rate!" He cites a middle-aged married couple earning $30,000 per year with two children. "Given the level of their federal marginal tax bracket, their loss, at the margin, of the Earned Income Tax Credit from earning extra income, and their exposure to marginal FICA taxation, their current total marginal effective tax on earning an extra dollar is 47.6 percent!"

There is another key element in the struggle to escape poverty that deserves mention: education expenses. Education costs at the primary, secondary, and higher-education levels are not taxed under the FairTax because they are considered investments in intellectual capital. That means that college and all the education costs on the way to college can be paid for using increased take-home pay and that such earnings *and expenditures* are not subject to any taxation by the federal government. This makes higher education more possible for all Americans, including the poor.

Today, tuition expense is not tax deductible. To pay $10,000 in college or other school tuition, a typical middle-class American must earn $15,540—and this number assumes that only federal income taxes and the employee payroll tax will be deducted from the gross pay. The amount one must earn to pay the $10,000 is really more like $20,120, once employer and state income taxes are taken into account. This represents a huge barrier to the middle class and an impossible one to the poor if scholarships are not available. But under the FairTax there are no taxes on income, so $10,000 earned can be used to pay $10,000 in tuition expenses—making education much more affordable. The FairTax makes education about half as expensive to American families, and that can mean a lot to those working to break out of poverty.

At the workplace, the FairTax removes the tax cost of upward mobility, making success far more likely and desirable. Let's consider a low-income American who has a dream of owning his own business. Most job growth, after all, comes in businesses of fewer than fifty people. Let's say our man dreams of opening a small landscape and yard services company. He buys a used pickup truck, lawnmowers, rakes, and trimmers, and hires two friends. Licenses are paid for. Door hangers are left throughout neighborhoods with likely potential clients. The business is off to a good start. That is, until the tax consequences come into focus.

For every dollar our entrepreneur pays to his workers, 7.65 cents must be paid to Uncle Sam for Social Security and Medicare. That's from the first dollar. The owner is also paying 15 cents on every dollar of his income off the top for his own Social Security and Medicare "self-employment tax." And that's before he pays his business and/or personal income taxes. And, of course, he still has to spend the time to get the right forms and account for those wages and profits to the federal government, because failure to report every penny can result in penalties, garnishment of wages or profits, seizure of property, and even jail time.

If the business takes off beyond all expectations, the self-employed owner can end up paying a 35 percent income-tax rate on top of his employees' FICA taxes. Welcome to success! You now can take home a bit more than 45 cents of each dollar you earn, though of course, you still have to leave some money to actually run your company. And please don't forget to devote some of what's left over to your kids' college funds and your retirement savings. Ready to offer health-care benefits or paid vacation to your workers? Many just say no, because they can't afford it. The regressive nature of the FICA tax and tax punishment of upward mobility put the American dream out of reach of too many Americans. That hurts us all.

Now let's start that business under the FairTax. The entrepreneur doesn't have to pay any federal tax on the purchase of that used pickup truck because the tax was paid when the truck was new and first purchased (the FairTax does not impose double taxation on used items). Additionally, the purchase is made with what under our current tax system is called pretax income—the owner's whole paycheck and savings free of taxes. There is also no employment tax levied on the entrepreneur for workers hired or for any supplies or equipment purchased for the business.

Under the FairTax, the business succeeds or fails based solely on how the company is run and the market is faring—not based on the tax system. Considering the fact that two-thirds of American jobs are created in small businesses, the advantages to those businesses of the FairTax are compelling. The worst thing that can be said about the FairTax's effect on small business is that those who make retail sales are required to collect and remit the tax. That, however, is not so different from their current responsibility to state and local taxing authorities, and under the FairTax, businesses get to keep a small percentage of the taxes collected for their trouble.

The Great American Middle Class

The GI Bill, which brought college education to average "dog-faces," and the American labor movement (unions) were two hugely important factors that allowed rapid growth of the middle class in the twentieth century. The former did so by creating a newly accessible path of education and professional opportunity and the latter by making collective bargaining a powerful lever to increase wages and benefits. While the rights of labor have been protected by the federal government and in our courts since then, our tax policies have undermined upward mobility. The fact that higher education costs keep rising and that such costs are largely paid for with debt secured by after-tax income doesn't help at all.

After the poor, the greatest beneficiaries of the FairTax are middle-class Americans. In 2008 the brilliant Boston University economist Laurence Kotlikoff examined in detail how a typical middle-class couple with a joint income, a house, retirement savings, and two kids would fare under the FairTax. Using an advanced financial-planning program, he found that such a family would "enjoy increases in their annual living standards ranging from 27.9 percent to 33.5 percent" because the taxes on their income and investments would be drastically reduced. No matter your thoughts on the current tax system, it's hard to argue with numbers like these.

Our zero-sum income-tax system has other vexing indirect consequences for the middle class. Under our current tax policies, the rich—those who make the greatest investment in the growth of the economy—must be dunned with higher taxes in order to reduce middle-class taxes. As a result, the investor class invests fewer dollars in job creation, which, in turn, hurts the middle class.

The economic downturn, which has so severely hurt the middle class, both in terms of lost savings and investments and in terms of historically high unemployment rates, is bad enough. But as more and more American businesses move manufacturing and service jobs offshore to escape the crippling tax consequences of operating at home, the middle class loses even more jobs. The income-tax system has proved very positive for call centers in India but is a slap in the face to American workers.

With each passing year, manufacturing has become an ever-decreasing part of the overall economy. Consider that the value of all goods manufactured in the United States was roughly 30 percent of the value of all goods and services in the economy. In 1953, 30 percent of our national economy came from manufacturing. It had dropped to 25 percent by 1970, 20 percent in 1982, and less than 15 percent in 2001. American jobs in manufacturing fell over the same period from more than 26 percent to about 10 percent. For union workers—or leaders—the effect of our income tax system on American jobs should come as a wake-up call.

NAFTA opened foreign markets to us and our markets to foreign competitors. The reasoning was that a rising sea of commerce lifts all boats. At first, experts predicted that only unskilled labor jobs would move abroad. But then went computer programmers, followed by the textile industry, the steel industry, electronic component manufacturers, lead pencil makers, and just about every other vulnerable American industry. We do enjoy more and more commerce with foreign nations since NAFTA, *and* we have lost more and more of our manufacturing and service base. Increasingly, our economy is based not on building things but on buying things. For most of us, this spells inevitable trouble.

The American automobile industry provides a perfect example of how outsourcing and increased dependence on foreign trade can negatively affect the entire American economy. The damage to our service and industry base became especially obvious during the financial crisis. The shock wave of the collapsed automobile industry resonated across our economic sea like a tsunami to affect all those manufacturers who supplied parts and labor to Detroit, as well as the banks, the real estate agents, the insurance and medical fields, the charities, and the grocery stores and restaurants, among other things that were supported and patronized by autoworkers who lost their jobs. Much has been made of the hourly wages offered and retirement benefits promised to foreign workers as compared to ours, but little has been said about tax policies that, by some estimates, add 20 percent or more to the cost of producing an automobile here. Our inability to remove hidden tax costs in order to equalize tax factors with offshore producers hurts everyone.

As I've already explained at length, the elimination of these taxes on American automobiles would not only reduce the cost of purchasing an American car but would also strengthen the automobile industry by making it more competitive with foreign producers. The FairTax makes the United States the only industrialized nation with a zero rate of tax on manufacturing. It will therefore act as a supermagnet to investment, leading to more and better paying jobs. It exempts all taxes from domestically manufactured goods that are exported, but levies an equal tax on imports, when sold here, creating a desperately needed level playing field for American producers who sell their goods here. The same effects apply to all the other employers in the United States, who see the bottom line benefit of not being taxed for growth, profits, or productivity. They will hire again and pay better wages and benefits when our economy is growing so fast that the worker is again in great demand. Higher wages and better benefits also ripple across the economic spectrum to every other activity that depends on commerce and an employed—and consuming— American workforce.

Senior Citizens

The FairTax ensures Social Security's soundness by funding it with a progressive, broad-based national retail sales tax rather than the current regressive, narrow payroll tax. According to Professor Dale Jorgenson of Harvard University's Economics Department, revenues to Social Security and Medicare would double as the size of the economy doubles within fifteen years after passage of the FairTax.

The FairTax repeals the taxation of Social Security benefits when a retiree decides to rejoin the workforce and adjusts Social

Security indexing to protect seniors. The prebate automatically adjusts, and the Social Security cost-of-living allowance (COLA) automatically adjusts to any increases in retail costs caused by the FairTax.

The FairTax ends *all* record keeping and income-tax filings of any kind for seniors, totally insulating them from the high costs and abusive tactics of tax preparers. The FairTax does not tax used goods, giving low-income seniors tax-free choices in what they buy. The FairTax reduces costs incurred by manufacturers, service providers, and retailers, allowing them to lower costs to seniors and all consumers. The FairTax eliminates tax penalties on IRA withdrawals and taxes levied on all other retirement investments as they grow. The FairTax ends gift and estate taxes, which penalize legitimate heirs, and eliminates the need for complex planning to minimize tax consequences when preparing a will. The FairTax allows seniors to sell their homes and pay no capital gains taxes. The FairTax generates an economic boom, which eases future budget pressure on seniors' entitlements. The FairTax ensures that seniors' grandchildren have the same opportunities they did, instead of a declining chance for advancement because so much of their earnings have already been spent. The FairTax prebate adjusts, as does the Social Security cost-of-living allowance, to all consumer costs, including medicines and other health-care expenses.

Investors

There are no capital gains taxes under the FairTax. That means that when investments are made, the federal government no longer receives part of the profits on those investments. The combination of increased investment in stocks and bonds, industry, and start-up businesses and the absence of punishment for successful risk taking in betting on growth will spur even more investment.

Millionaires and billionaires will pay the 23 percent rate on consumption when they purchase goods and services; their existing wealth will be taxed when spent. Additionally, under the FairTax taxes are equalized by rate but the system takes more from those who spend more. This corrects the situation pointed out, to his credit, by Warren Buffett, one of the wealthiest men in the world: that his secretary pays a higher tax rate on her salary than he does on millions of dollars of dividend and investment income.

The wealthy should not despair about the FairTax but rather embrace it, because the growth of their wealth through investment and savings will no longer be punished, nor will the government be able to take the legacies they leave for their heirs. For senior citizens, serious investors, and everyone else who relies increasingly on investments for retirement income and security, this is a healthy and much-needed change.

The Environmental Movement—Another FairTax Winner

One of the great ideological and scientific debates that divides the nation is between those who accept global warming as the effect of human action on the natural world and those who attribute such change to the natural cycles of warming and cooling that occur as our planet wobbles slightly on its axis.

To most scientists, the evidence is clear-cut and ominous and the need for change immediate. But most skeptics consider it a huge mistake to dramatically reduce industrial and technological activities to accommodate a small change that, they believe, is really caused by the typical cycles of nature, not by the destructive actions of man. In any case, for the last twenty years we have taught every schoolchild about animal species that are disappearing, ice shelves that are melting, and the steps that individuals can take to mitigate the damage.

I have been brought along to this perspective by my young sons and have a hard time understanding why some political leaders and pundits don't recognize at the very least the sea change in perception that is occurring among younger generations. In my home we recycle faithfully, and although I drive a big car that can handle too-frequent street flooding in my sea-level hometown of Houston, my wife drives a hybrid vehicle. (I get the kids when it floods.) We reason, perhaps disingenuously, that we balance each other out to create one ecologically sensitive person.

But regardless of your thoughts on climate change, any new tax on consumption will make people think twice about whether they really need a brand-new whatever when the old one still works perfectly well. The experts predict that consumption will actually pick up as people take home more money after the second year of the FairTax, but it is worth noting that more used goods will be purchased and then resold later because there is no FairTax on used items.

In this respect the FairTax represents a useful and frugal reminder that a new kind of recycling can have a healthy and financially beneficial effect on our consuming mentality. Will dishcloths become more popular than paper towels? Probably not. But there is every reason to believe that we will all think a little more about our consumption choices with the FairTax and will use items until they are no longer useful and consider buying used items rather than new. And that's undoubtedly healthy for our environment, our pocketbooks, and our future.

Chapter 7   **The Recession-Proof Income-Tax Industry**

"When the people find they can vote themselves money, that will herald the end of the republic."

—Benjamin Franklin

T HE DAMAGE THAT the income-tax system does to the engines of prosperity in the United States should provide all the reason necessary to throw this weighty albatross off the neck of the American economy. And yet, although experts and average taxpayers alike point to the dysfunction of the system, the idea of creating something better has failed to gain much traction in Washington, D.C. Why?

Despite exclamations from nearly every politician that "something must be done" about the complexity of the income-tax system, year after year the tax code only becomes more and more complicated. For most people, these promises of simplification no longer mean much because the opposite so often proves true.

Since the last great simplification effort during the Reagan years, when the number of income brackets was reduced to three, the tax code has seen more than sixteen thousand changes. With so many changes, the code becomes not only harder to understand but also easier to corrupt. How is this possible? How can such a universally despised creation of our elected representatives be so immune to simple corrections at one end of the public-policy spectrum and fundamental reform at the other?

Simply stated, the immediate self-interest of Congress, tax lobbyists, and the culture that has grown up around the tax committees is why the tax code never improves. Too many in Washington have a stake in warfare over taxes, the profits derived from the process of granting tax breaks, and the power of the tax-writing committees to pick winners and losers.

The primary beneficiaries of our tax code are, in truth, a small group of elected officials, advocates, and lobbyists who profit from manipulating, researching, and opining on the tax code. The current system makes lobbyists rich, academicians important, and members of Congress powerful. It gives "tax reform" groups an almost eternal purpose and an unending funding base. What is very good for probably no more than one hundred thousand people in Washington is the tail that wags the national dog when it comes to tax policy. It is self-interest and corruption raised to a level of sophistication that provides only the illusion of respectability and real purpose. In a sense, the political elite represent a new American *aristocracy*, divorced from the effect of their work on the populace and wholly focused on profit and power.

For those yearning for bipartisan cooperation in Washington, the daily selling off of the income-tax code and unreasoning resistance to any reform may, sadly, be the very best evidence of true bipartisan cooperation inside the Washington beltway. Efforts to reform the income-tax system meet with cold shoulders from both sides of the fence. It's as good an example as can be found of the distance between Washington, D.C., and hometown America. Put another way, the few in Congress who surround congressional tax-writing committees have put their own narrow interest in power and profit ahead of the best interests of the nation.

While Americans suffer from the damaged economy, things have never looked brighter in Washington, D.C. "Gucci gulch" is the nickname for the hallway outside the hearing room of the tax-writing House Ways and Means Committee in the Longworth House Office Building. It refers to the expensive designer shoes favored by well-heeled tax lobbyists.

Special-interest groups spend more than $1 billion a year on trying to win tax breaks for favored clients. In Washington, lobbying has become the most lucrative business in town. Like the gold rushers of the nineteenth century, these lobbyists have found rich pickings mining the House Ways and Means Committee, where tax laws are set. It is a bipartisan exercise in congressional self-interest that has very little to do with the economic health of the nation and everything to do with the unique Washington power industry that surrounds the federal tax system.

With more than $2.5 trillion of tax revenues received each year, every new loophole, favor, policy, or gimmick developed by these lobbyists is like a flake, nugget, or vein of gold. While most taxpayers and businesses suffer from the complexity of the tax code, those who win exceptions for wealthy clients have become the richest and most successful lobbyists in Washington. It is a recession-proof industry because people are always looking for tax breaks, and in fact, the tougher times get, the more desperate companies become to find ways to reduce tax costs.

In this way, the complexity of the tax code provides a source of power and wealth for those who make a living trying to manipulate it. Those elected officials and staff members who serve on the exclusive House Ways and Means Committee, Senate Finance Committee, and Joint Committee on Taxation live at the pinnacle of power over the tax code because they develop and grant the favors, gimmicks, loopholes, and arcane provisions that have come to define our national tax system. These members of Congress are driven to defend the income-tax system not by ideology but by the entirely human desire for power and importance.

Bluff and gruff House Ways and Means chairman Charlie Rangel, Harlem's representative, is the very picture of the ward-heeling politician of old. When one blogger confronted him in 2009 with a video camera to ask why taxpayers had to subsidize his limo service, Rangel's friend-to-all smile turned sour and he asked, "Why don't you mind your own damned business?" The blogger, along with many others, felt that our tax dollars and how they are used are indeed the business of American citizens. Mr. Rangel might have been feeling a bit sensitive that day, as he had recently joined the Washington, D.C., "million-dollar club." That's a "club" for those who have spent at least a million dollars in campaign contributions and personal funds for a legal defense.

Mr. Rangel was caught avoiding paying taxes on his income from a luxury condo in the Caribbean. He said he didn't understand the tax implications of that income. His explanation was a masterful example of how to "accept" responsibility while shifting the blame to others: "While over the years I delegated to my staff the completion of my annual House financial disclosure statements, I had the ultimate responsibility. . . . I sincerely regret and take personal responsibility for these errors," he said.

"I personally feel that I have done nothing morally wrong." Mr. Rangel is also being investigated for his use of four rent-stabilized apartments at New York City's Lenox Terrace and for trading favorable tax treatment for donations to the Charles B. Rangel Center for Public Service at City College of New York—which was built with a $1.9 million earmark.

Public service has been very rewarding for Mr. Rangel, who recently amended his personal wealth reports, having "found" investments and income that make him worth somewhere between $1.5 million and $2.5 million. From humble beginnings he, like so many others in Congress and those who work near the centers of congressional power, jealously guards the royal treatment that delivers perks, investment opportunities, a lot of cash, and an elevated standard of living that is "above" the life of mere American citizens. We have, somehow, allowed royalty back into a nation founded on the premise that all citizens, including those who governed, are equal.

If you were wondering how strong the self-interest is in Washington that protects and perpetuates the income-tax system, wonder no more. There is a real sense of entitlement on the tax-writing committees by members of both parties. There is also acceptance in Washington that such power and spoils are the rightful rewards of those with such power. It makes even more remarkable the fact that the original and enduring sponsor of the FairTax legislation, Representative John Linder of Georgia, serves on the powerful House Ways and Means committee. As my grandfather used to say, "Honor dies where interest lies." Mr. Linder is the codicil to that axiom: "Honor is also born where interest lies."

Both Republicans and Democrats relish the heady power over so much money—about $2.5 trillion a year in tax receipts. They have the power not only to grant favors to rich and powerful supplicants but to punish political opponents, make lobbyists rich, and make average Americans and businesses behave differently through incentives and punishments written into the tax code. There have been more than sixteen thousand changes to the tax code since Ronald Reagan's reform of the system in the eighties; that means we have seen an average of about three changes to the tax code every day Congress has been in session. There is simply no good reason for legislators to "check and balance" the damaging effects of these changes on the average taxpayer and the tax code itself. They have power reminiscent of an ancient aristocracy, and it represents an almost irresistible self-interest that, in the worldview of most in Washington, eclipses the damage the system causes and the best interests of the nation.

Perhaps not surprisingly, the ranks of tax lobbyists who work for businesses and individuals seeking favored tax treatment are constantly replenished by former House and Senate staffers and members of Congress. "Hundreds of former members of Congress and staffers who leave Congress go through the revolving door to lobby the people they used to work for," says Dave Levinthal, the communications director of the Center for Responsive Politics. Its Web site at OpenSecrets.org contains a wealth of information that pulls the curtain away from the worst influence peddling in Washington. Even that sunlight has done little to slow the tendency of those with government power over the citizenry to profit and further expand the ranks of the new American political elite.

Among many others, Vin Weber, once a powerful Minnesota congressman, is now considered one of the most influential Republican lobbyists in the capital. Thomas Hale Boggs of Patton Boggs is the son of Hale Boggs, a former Democratic House majority leader, and is said to wield more power than any elected official. Former senator Bob Dole, Democratic powerhouse Tony Podesta, Linda Daschle, and name after recognizable name now work their former colleagues and family connections on behalf of special interests. Just ask former congressmen like Bill Paxon of New York and Bob Livingston of Louisiana, now lobbyists who, according to Washingtonian. com, can earn their annual congressional salary of $165,200 representing a single client. Their lobbying firm made $16 million in 2008, mostly from the very Louisiana interests who were once constituents.

DLA Piper rivals competitor Patton Boggs as one of the largest lobbying firms in Washington. It saw $46 million in lobbying revenues in 2008 and has employed such former congressional powerhouses as former House leaders Dick Armey, a Republican, and Dick Gephardt, and former Senate majority leader George Mitchell, both powerful and well-known Democrats. These firms represent the real power behind the curtain and are less concerned about partisan causes than about the lucrative fees and the ability to shape public policy. These are the entirely human pursuits that unify the political elite *of both parties* in Washington: money and power. Mr. Armey, in fact, is an active proponent of Steve Forbes's "flat tax," which although far simpler than the income-tax system, preserves the role of tax lobbyists in Washington.

In one final, revealing example, consider former Louisiana senator John Breaux and former Florida senator Connie Mack, who headed the bipartisan blue-ribbon president's commission on tax reform in 2005. They were tasked by President Bush with suggesting ways to simplify the tax code and make other improvements. The commission deliberated for months, heard testimony from many, including FairTax proponent Americans for Fair Taxation. They received thousands of pages of FairTax research, in fact—and ignored it all. Instead, the commission quietly created its own version of a national consumption tax, loaded it with exceptions and deductions (preserving the tax lobbyists' role and driving up the tax rate necessary for the system to function), and then announced to the public and the media that a national consumption tax had been studied (everyone assumed they meant the FairTax), it was unworkable, and the rate would have to be too high. Shortly after concluding their "independent" work, the commissioners took positions with high-powered D.C. lobbying firms, as did many on the staff. If you conclude the fix was in you are absolutely right. If you are wondering why—just remember human personal motivations.

It is not uncommon for a House staffer with five to ten years' experience overseeing one arcane section of the tax code or a given industry to go on to earn a six- to seven-figure "signing bonus" with one of several K Street tax lobbying firms. It is a rich reward commonly planned on by those staffers fortunate enough to find work on these committees. In Washington, these jobs are the surest path to personal wealth after toiling long hours for years in a place that is marked by political intrigues, power struggles, and the absence of laws that check things like abusive employment practices. A sharp mind, an appetite for opportunity, and the ruthless determination to survive and advance in what has been called the "last plantation" on Capitol Hill can lead tax staffers to lucrative rewards in the tax lobbying industry.

The thought of a tax system that eliminates this industry is not only unthinkable to many such staffers but an assault on personal plans for wealth and payment for years of sacrifices made. These staffers, the unelected legislators in Washington, work closely with those who defend the system against change and often earn as much as $250,000 a year in salaries. Even before landing those dream lobbying jobs that may be years ahead—staffers find rich rewards at these richest of all congressional committees. For those readers struggling to make mortgage payments, it is sobering to learn the details of six-figure staff salaries and generous bonuses granted on tax writing congressional committees.

A small part of the academic world is just as guilty of perpetuating the income-tax system. A small circle of economists and other tax experts have learned the tax code as well as or better than the people who write the tax laws. The distributional effects of taxes, the revenues collected, the accepted protocols for estimates, and the context and history of changes to the tax code make these academics the high priests of the system, who routinely attack as simple heresy any attempt to change or improve the labyrinthine structure they know so well. For example, William G. Gale, a critic of the FairTax, heads the Tax Policy Center and is a knowledgeable income-tax expert and economist who once worked on the Council of Economic Advisers. Mr. Gale and a host of others specialize in the income tax code, its history, and the factions that advocate changes to benefit a particular philosophy or constituency. It's hard to imagine someone whose career depends on the income tax advocating any sort of change to the system that makes his or her expertise and opinion less valuable. Mr. Gale and others who are so valued in Washington tax circles never, ever, publically embrace a wholesale replacement of the system for entirely understandable reasons.

Specialized publications like the respected *Tax Notes* cater to this audience of tax lawyers, policy advocates, lobbyists, academicians, and tax policy makers. Without the tax code, the hierarchy disappears. This is why finding an "objective" opinion about fundamental changes to our tax system is so difficult; most tax experts rely upon the very system they are asked to analyze for both their incomes and standing in the Washington pecking order of influence and power.

Next, let's add those who believe they enjoy a tax-code advantage or whose work is based on navigating the tax code. The National Association of Realtors, for example, very strongly believes that the home mortgage deduction is a government subsidy upon which the sale of homes depends. The fact that a little more than 30 percent of the taxpaying public files the long form allowing tax deductions for interest payments makes little difference to their perspective. The fact that the FairTax delivers 100 percent of one's gross pay (minus state tax withholding or health-care or retirement deductions, of course) makes even less difference to this special-interest lobby.

The argument that it is better for a third of the population of homeowners to be able to deduct a fraction of their interest payments rather than everyone in the population gaining a pretax income status is nonsensical. But to paraphrase and apply Newton's laws to American politics, a policy in motion remains in motion without a countervailing force applied. The NAR didn't win the home interest deduction as a taxpayer subsidy to spur home sales growth; the deduction is simply what is left of the original concept that interest payments on debt should not be subject to federal taxation. But with the deduction established, the National Association of Realtors, more than one hundred thousand strong, is loath to give it up and issues dire warnings on the effect of the loss of this government subsidy on home ownership. It's a claim worth examining, as this is perhaps the best-known tax deduction. Also, considering the fact that most home sales are used homes, not new, their position would seem to be at odds with the vast majority of Realtors who would broker the sale or purchase of FairTax-free used homes.

Retailers dependent on the sale of foreign products unburdened by American tax costs voice similar objections to the FairTax without much thought for what such a policy does to American manufacturing and job creation. Other interest groups that understand and successfully manipulate the system of quid pro quo in Washington voice reservations about a new approach that may eliminate their perceived advantages over the rest of us.

Finally come the tax-reform and tax-advocacy groups that, paradoxically, only advocate for reform of the system they, too, have come to know so well. The endless fight for one provision or policy or another produces permanent jobs for people ranging from the tax arm of the AFL-CIO to Grover Norquist of Americans for Tax Reform. Without these debates over tax policy, these people would not have jobs.

Because the system is so ripe for manipulation and so rife with opportunities to choose who will win and who will lose, most tax-reform groups privately loathe the idea of any new federal tax system that ends their work by eliminating all of the loopholes, gimmicks, and potential for class warfare and manipulation of citizen and business behavior. Publicly, those on the right will profess in practiced "Washington-speak" that any reform is good, and they are seemingly benign about the growing FairTax phenomenon, though very few advocate on its behalf. They take active steps out of the public eye to frustrate progress on the FairTax within Washington policy circles.

Along with the profiteers feeding on the broken tax code there are responsible and hardworking experts who simply tell us what is happening to our taxes and in the committees. I have great respect for those at the Tax Foundation and in other organizations who earn reasonable salaries doing important work analyzing and communicating the picture of what the tax code and the army of lobbyists really do. The Center for Responsive Politics has done invaluable work, for example, exposing the growth of lobbyist influence and the revolving door that defines retirement options between Capitol Hill and the White House and the lucrative next chapter after "public service."

One might expect that the fourth estate, those reporters and editors who attend every hearing and who follow the culture surrounding the tax code, would expose the occasional tax bill provision that favors a single individual, ham-handed attempts to force behavior outcomes (which have backfired spectacularly), or the transitions of individuals from the congressional committees to the ranks of the tax lobbyists, but this is not the case.

The moves from staff to lobbying offices are perhaps routinely reported as professional advancement in the *Washington Post*, but the stink that should accompany such moves is all but lost on the inured noses of reporters, who simply see such moves, favors, and insider games as part of the normal process. To be fair, there have been articles in national publications, for example, on Ways and Means chairman Charlie Rangel's recent legal troubles. But such stories about a highly prominent figure reveal only the very tip of a massive iceberg of legalized favor trading that exists beneath the surface of public scrutiny. As sometimes happens when journalists cover powerful institutions, many have become so close to the inner and highly technical workings of the committees that they have become a part of the process and culture instead of detached observers or watchdogs reporting on how the machinations of these committees, lobbyists, and experts affect the common good.

As just one example, the collapse of the savings-and-loan industry in the mid-eighties, partly precipitated by dramatic and politically inspired changes to the tax code that had a disastrous effect on banks—and the American taxpayer—came as a complete surprise to these Washington-based journalists, pundits, and editors. It's only human. In the power culture of Washington, D.C., the rich and powerful attract friends in columnists, pundits, and journalists, and the culture and workings of such power have been accepted as the norm.

Chapter 8 **Doubts About the FairTax**

N DEBATING THE FairTax, some critics have adopted the mistaken position that because it is not perfect, it must be rejected. They ask, Why should we change our current system—no matter how destructive it is—to something that still has its own set of kinks? I said it before: perfection might be found in church or the smile of a child, but it can't be found in any national tax system. The only way to measure the worthiness of the FairTax system is to compare the full measure of the strengths and weaknesses of what is proposed with the overall weight of the strengths and weaknesses of the current system. Taken as a whole, it is hard to defend the current system's destructive effects or conclude that the FairTax is not far better.

I don't fault honest skepticism and believe FairTax proponents should take a far more tolerant view of such doubts. It is fair and, indeed, responsible to question the assumptions, cal-

ıy that underlie any proposed federal
I decided to dedicate a section of this
elf-interested supporters of the income
the last chapter, from legitimate doubt-

mple criticisms and work our way up to
ıments against the FairTax.

Loss of the Home Mortgage Interest Deduction

One of the biggest myths about our current tax system is that
the home mortgage interest deduction encourages home ownership among people who would not otherwise be able to afford
it. The truth is, countries without a home mortgage deduction
have no lower home-ownership rates than we have here in the
United States. As Harvard economists Edward L. Glaeser and
Jesse M. Shapiro wrote in a study they conducted in 2002,
"While the deduction appears to increase the amount spent on
housing, it appears to have almost no effect on the homeowner-
ship rate." But the mortgage interest deduction is nevertheless
an article of faith elevated to almost mythical proportions by
the National Association of Realtors. The truth is, the home
mortgage deduction was something of an accident.

At one time all interest payments on debt were considered
off limits for federal taxation and were instead allowed to be
deducted by taxpayers from their annual income subject to
taxation. As Roger Lowenstein brilliantly observed in the *New
York Times* some years ago, the interest deduction was probably
aimed at business payments on existing debt, and the home interest deduction just hitched a ride on that train, helping to
create the legend that this deduction was intended by Congress

to help people buy homes and that it, in fact, has that effect. It does not.

In truth, it helps people buy bigger homes than they could otherwise afford, and it helps richer people sell their bigger homes for more money. Only three out of ten taxpayers actually see any benefit from the home mortgage interest deduction, because most people file the IRS short form, which does not allow this calculation. The long form allows for mortgage interest deductions and other deductions, but most people consider the time and work required to fill out this form unjustified given the slight, if any, reduction they see in their annual tax bill. For the 30 percent who do fill out the long form, the savings on taxes owed are certainly important, but not that substantial: less than $2,000 per return.

Again, according to Lowenstein, the total of all those tax savings amounts to a pretty big number: about $76 billion a year off owed taxes in 2007. More than half of that saved tax cost is enjoyed by less than 12 percent of homeowners—and this 12 percent of Americans are people with incomes of more than $100,000 a year.

In the same year, the House Ways and Means Committee championed legislation that made the interest paid on credit cards no longer deductible. Remember that policy shift? No, you probably don't, because like so many things Congress does to raise taxes on everyone, this one got little attention before it happened and saw almost no advocacy on behalf of the average taxpayer.

And by the way, the same tax legislation also set the stage for the collapse of the savings-and-loan industry, which cost Americans about $160 billion in more debt. You see, the Ways and Means Committee dramatically changed the definition of the value of existing real estate by changing the tax write-off available on such holdings. When it did, banks were thrust overnight into violation of banking regulations requiring certain cash-to-loan ratios. That change cost not only banks but the American taxpayer billions of dollars in bailout costs to save the banks that failed. It's an aside, but a revealing one, on the damage that politics can wreak on the economy and taxpayers.

The real point I want to make about the mortgage deduction is that the FairTax does away with this deduction but provides something much better. The mortgage deduction today gives one out of three homeowners *some* money off taxes. The FairTax allows each American to take home not part of his or her earnings in a refund but all that he or she earns when it is earned. In other words, is it better to take home everything you earn or get back a fraction of the cost of the interest on your home loan?

"TRUE COST" OF HOUSING

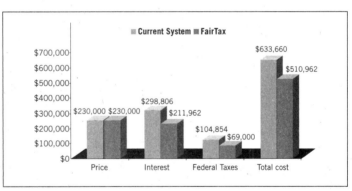

Source: Americans for Fair Taxation.

The FairTax is better for existing homeowners, better for renters, and better for potential home buyers. In addition to letting you take home your entire paycheck, the FairTax will reduce new-home costs by eliminating embedded costs of up to 20 percent. That means that new homes will cost less and be paid for with increased take-home pay. Plus, there is no FairTax collected on the sale of used homes, because that would represent double taxation. This is a boon for first-time home buyers, who typically buy a used home, and for every seller. For the vast majority of Americans already owning homes, this policy is a great benefit in both purchases and sales. Instead of a modest deduction that benefits one-third of the homeowner population, the FairTax delivers a larger benefit to every American.

Charitable Giving

Right now, Congress wants to reduce the amount of the deduction that higher earners receive when giving to charities, but the FairTax has no such deduction. Some worry this will dissuade people from contributing to worthy charitable causes, but the FairTax research says it best—truly generous people choose how much to give based on how much money is left in their pockets after the government has taken its piece.

According to a study conducted by the Beacon Hill Institute of Boston for the FairTax campaign, charitable donations would increase by approximately 0.89 percent (compared with the rate of contribution if the current system continues) immediately after the FairTax is enacted and would further increase by 2.4 percent within ten years and 4.99 percent after twenty years.

The study also notes that under President Reagan, when the top tax rate decreased from 70 percent to 28 percent between 1980 and 1986, charitable contributions increased from $48.7 billion to $93.7 billion. This occurred even though the cost of giving increased for itemizing taxpayers.

The 23 Percent Tomato or the 30 Percent Tomato?

Despite the efforts of Americans for Fair Taxation to dispel any misunderstanding about the way the FairTax is calculated, this is the main argument that some critics use to show that the FairTax is not all it's cracked up to be. When expressed as sales taxes are normally calculated, the FairTax is a 30 percent tax on new goods and services. When expressed as income taxes are normally calculated, it is a 23 percent tax. This has led some critics to charge dishonesty in promoting the FairTax as a 23 percent rate.

Income taxes are expressed as the percentage rate of the tax when both the tax and the income are first combined. Sales taxes, on the other hand, are normally calculated exclusive of the tax on the retail price. The two calculations are, appropriately, described as "inclusive" and "exclusive." As I explained earlier, the difference between the two lies only in the way the amount is expressed—like the difference between measuring something in centimeters and measuring it in inches.

It is somewhat vexing to proponents of the FairTax that income-tax defenders insist on expressing income taxes *inclusively* but only compare these rates to FairTaxes calculated *exclusively*. Income-tax rates can only be compared fairly with FairTax rates and annual tax burdens by using the same method of calculation for both. Most taxpayers have become used to an inclusive method of tax-rate computation. Here is how inclusive rates translate to exclusive: 15 percent inclusive = 18 percent exclusive; 20 percent inclusive = 25 percent exclusive; 25 percent inclusive = 33 percent exclusive; 33 percent inclusive = 50 percent exclusive.

To make such a comparison complete, readers should also consider that to truly calculate current income-tax burdens, one must also include FICA payroll taxes. To make matters even more complicated, remember that our income taxes are paid at different rates according to different levels of earnings. This is what is meant by the "marginal" tax rates: under the income-tax system we pay a higher tax rate on the last dollar earned than on the first dollar earned. Excise taxes and user fees collected by the federal government are, of course, also part of our tax costs, such as the tax added to the price of a gallon of gasoline or an airline ticket, but we can dispense with these amounts when discussing the FairTax because these taxes would still exist under the FairTax.

Take Home Your Whole Paycheck

In what I have already written above and in speeches by every FairTaxer you will hear that the FairTax allows you to take home your whole paycheck, free of federal withholding or payroll taxes. FairTax critics take issue with this claim because health-care insurance payments, retirement contributions automatically deducted from paychecks, state income taxes and other local taxes automatically withheld, and even child-support payments that are withheld will not change after enactment of the FairTax. In this respect, the critics are right.

The FairTax eliminates all *federal* withholding and payroll taxes from paychecks. On one end of the earning spectrum—for those who currently have no federal income taxes withheld—the FairTax would increase take-home pay by 7.65 percent through the elimination of Social Security and Medicare taxes. On the other end of the earnings spectrum, a self-employed person in a 35 percent tax bracket, with no deductions, will see close to a 50 percent increase in take-home pay. Of course, I should also point out that almost 4 percent of federal government revenues now come from excise taxes and fees. These will remain even after the FairTax, so one cannot say that *all* federal taxes on the poor are eliminated—just *almost* all.

The "Free Lunch" and Revenue Neutrality

How can the federal government take in the same amount of revenues under the FairTax if most taxpayers are paying far less and "embedded" income-tax costs are eliminated?

Simply stated, there is no "free lunch" wherein new revenues magically appear out of thin air under the FairTax. But the revenue base is expanded when twelve to twenty million illegal immigrants pay federal taxes as consumers, when those profiting in the $2 trillion annual underground economy pay taxes as consumers, when loopholes are eliminated, and when existing wealth is taxed when spent. The cost of obeying income-tax rules is also added to this side of the balance sheet, producing hundreds of billions of dollars more in savings.

But to be fair, I must also recognize that the FairTax eliminates existing revenue sources that have been overlooked in promoting the FairTax in the past. Sure, federal taxes on income are replaced with taxes on spending. That's clear. But what about those embedded tax costs? Those are eliminated, too. Does that not really mean that those in the underground economy are already paying some of the tax burden? Well, yes, it does.

If we accept that embedded tax costs amount to as much as 20 percent of the retail price of American products, we must also conclude that when the drug dealers, prostitutes, gamblers, and others who deal under the table purchase goods under the

FairTax their spending—and taxes paid—will not mean an entirely new source of revenue. Right now a drug dealer pays no income taxes on his earnings, but he does carry some of the costs of the federal government whenever he purchases goods with embedded costs.

Embedded Taxes—Do They Exist?

To many macroeconomists embedded taxes are a fiction or have little or no effect on the overall economy. But ask almost anyone working at the micro level, and the theories that define macroeconomics seem equally myopic. Most business owners will tell you that the 7.65 percent tax on employees' wages is certainly a cost of doing business. They will go on to tell you that corporate taxes are a constant reminder of the cost of government on businesses and that tax-compliance costs can be very high, as filings must be made on time, paperwork developed and stored properly, and, occasionally, audit expenses incurred. For big business and the truly wealthy, add the discretionary but often effective cost of tax lobbyists and tax lawyers to chart out prudent strategies for winning tax breaks or minimizing tax liabilities. Some experts have argued that the use of such strategies is so common that the true corporate tax rate is not 35 percent but closer to 15 percent or 20 percent.

But it is also true that many FairTax advocates have misunderstood the research of Harvard economist Dale Jorgenson describing embedded tax costs. In some cases these costs do not necessarily increase retail prices but instead come out of employee wages and benefits. Higher tax costs may also mean that fewer dollars are spent on research or that plans to expand are put on hold.

Because there are many largely unstudied effects on business behavior caused by embedded tax costs, we cannot know for certain that all retail prices will fall under the FairTax. That all prices will fall up to 23 percent and all wages will rise an equal amount is the "free lunch" argument, and it does not hold water. On the other hand, those who argue that retail prices will remain the same after enactment of the FairTax, even without embedded costs, are mistaken. Even if prices rise somewhat under the FairTax, it is important to remember that no American will pay more than 23 percent of his or her spending on this new tax, that most people will pay less than that amount out of total discretionary spending, and that all purchases will be made with what is today considered pretax, or gross, income. Some have argued that retail prices may go up as much as 15 to 17 percent with the FairTax added. In the absence of further study on the effect of retail prices, these critics should not be easily dismissed. But even if they are right, we still enjoy a far more favorable tax and job creation environment with the FairTax.

It is equally wrong to claim that where retail prices can fall because of elimination of tax costs, competitive pressures won't squeeze the higher prices out of the marketplace. There is, of course, a desire by all businesses to increase profits, but there is also sound and prudent fear of losing market share to competitors selling similar products and services for lower prices.

Another hotly debated element of the "embedded tax cost" arguments involves how much of eliminated tax costs will go to employers and how much will go to employees. I like the commonsense answer that since the FairTax ends the FICA payroll tax, employees will keep their contribution and employers will keep their contribution. Adding up the totals, employers will see an elimination of corporate taxes of up to 35 percent of profits, the employer's share of FICA taxes, which amounts to 7.65 percent of payroll costs (up to $102,500 of each employee's earnings), and a portion of the 2.65 percent of employees' earnings over $102,500 annually. They will also see income-tax compliance costs fall, though retailers will see additional costs incurred for collecting and remitting FairTax amounts (though they will receive a 0.25 percent fee for their trouble).

Some critics of the FairTax assail proponents for claiming that, with the elimination of FICA, employee wages will go up. I don't believe that a hiring agreement where the employer and the employee agree on, say, a salary of $60,000 a year can be construed after enactment of the FairTax to mean that the employee now takes home $60,000 a year minus his or her own FICA tax contribution. Nor do I believe that under the Fair-Tax an employer should be required to pay over to the employee, above and beyond the agreed salary ($60,000 a year in our example), the amount that the employer now contributes in FICA taxes.

The bottom line is somewhere between what opponents and proponents commonly claim about both wages and retail prices after the FairTax. Wages won't likely go higher than agreed gross pay before the FairTax, as a matter of simple calculation, nor will retail prices drop far enough that consumers see a huge reduction. What will happen is that paychecks will be far fatter, tax costs will be made visible, embedded costs will be eliminated, allowing price reductions, and business decisions will no longer depend on tax considerations. And while retail prices may not fall the full amount of embedded tax costs in every case, it is likely that a growing economy and elimination of these costs will produce higher wages and better benefits, growth in the job market, and a healthier economy in both the short and the long run.

Chapter 9   **The FairTax Will Not Be Enacted Without Overwhelming Citizen Pressure**

"Our federal tax system is, in short, utterly impossible, utterly unjust and completely counterproductive. [It] reeks with injustice and is fundamentally un-American. . . . It has earned a rebellion and it's time we rebelled."
                                        —Ronald Reagan

I F I HAVE done my job and convinced you that America needs the FairTax, you might be wondering, "How can the FairTax win enactment?" The answer is both simple and hard: it will only come one congressional district at a time—with each step forward reinforcing the grassroots work of others. The larger answer is that only the full participation of the American body politic has the power to overcome the entrenched interests in Washington, D.C., that surround the income-tax system.

The good news—and bad news—is that the benefits of the income-tax system are largely confined to a ridiculously small number of extremely influential people in and around Congress, while the disadvantages and destructive effects of direct taxation affect the entire nation. Implicit in such strategy questions are two more fundamental questions: can the anonymous *many* overcome the politically powerful *few* and, most significantly, does our form of democracy still work when the majority's interest requires change or sacrifice by the political elite? The FairTax is, seen in this light, nothing less than a test of the fundamental promise of the Framers' vision of a representative democracy.

We, the people, essentially have to run over the tax lobbyists and all their friends for the FairTax to see enactment. This is no small task and one that the political class routinely dismisses as unrealistic. True, one cannot ever overestimate the clout this crowd will bring to bear in defense of the lucrative federal system that allows favor trading, huge profits, loophole buying and selling, and the understandable social networking that this significant industry produces. Academicians, legislators, lobbyists, and even tax-reform groups and think tanks all feed off the dysfunction and corruption of the income-tax system and have—and will—resist this needed and sensible reform.

The merits of a tax system that unleashes our potential for invention, competition, productivity, and investment are not, alone, sufficient to win Congress away from its own self-interests or to overcome the very human resistance to change. Even the potential of the FairTax to solve the current economic crisis by restoring consumer confidence, allowing distressed homeowners the increased take-home pay to satisfy mortgage obligations, and attract a predicted $10–15 trillion of foreign investment into our economy does not trump the power and profit motives of income-tax defenders.

The FairTax effort has already suffered attacks (in races from Arizona to Texas to Georgia) from political operatives who distort the issue for political advantage, ignore the considerable research that has been accomplished, and even (in the case of one well-known income-tax lobbyist, Bruce Bartlett) falsely attribute the genesis of the FairTax to a religious group in nationally read publications.

In recent elections for Representative Pete Olson in Texas and Senator Saxby Chambliss in Georgia, the FairTax attack ads either had little effect or, as in the election in Georgia, back-fired. In Arizona, the head of the state Democratic Party au-thored ads and direct mail attacking pro-FairTax candidates as seeking huge new tax increases (leaving out elimination of the income tax, of course) and did real damage to their campaigns.

Political operatives who once found a safe tactic in attacking the FairTax have made the mistake of underestimating the growing grassroots strength of the FairTax movement in some parts of the country where the FairTax is well understood. It's understandable. The issue is a case in point of the distance (and disconnect) between the citizen and the political class of elites when it comes to who really benefits from the income-tax sys-tem. In this, the political class can only continue profiting from a clearly destructive system by obscuring the reality of such damage and by avoiding the most fundamental tenet of our form of government—self-rule by our citizens. These opera-tives and candidates have come to rely on their ability to distort the issue to advance their fortunes.

To achieve the red-hot heat necessary to overcome such self-interest, a far greater number of our citizens must become aware of the details of the FairTax, their immediate self-interest in the idea, and the harm that the income-tax system produces for us today and for our children in the future.

Only when members of Congress face daily hectoring, the loss of voter support, and imminent defeat will the FairTax reach the floor of the House. That kind of intense citizen pressure has not yet been achieved, but grassroots strength is steadily grow-ing toward that day, and in pockets of the nation as in Georgia this intense citizen demand exists today. When we finally see the FairTax campaign reach the tipping point, the status-quo crowd (this will include both Democrats and Republicans) will give in to citizen pressure—*and* almost inevitably call for a destructive legislative modification of the FairTax.

This modification will take the form of a floor amendment to exempt some item—probably a food, medicine, or service—from the FairTax. It will sound eminently reasonable to exempt, say, baby food from the FairTax, but through this one amendment, the door will be reopened for continued congressional mischief to punish and reward and to preserve the role of the tax lobbyist.

In the case of this floor debate, FairTax supporters will have a matter of hours to raise constituent pressure to the boiling point and shut down wholly predictable congressional attempts to retain power over the tax system and the freedom to self-deal that so corrupt the system today. The mechanics of this citizen response will require a large presence in Washington during the debate, an e-mail network that can be quickly alerted to mischief in a call to action, and a phone- and fax-based Paul Revere–style network that will produce citizen pressure sufficient to overwhelm congressional offices both in Washington and in home districts. The same fight will occur in the Senate.

For the constitutional amendment fight, the timing will be easier, but the goal of winning two-thirds of the entire Congress to support the legislation will be more difficult. Without doubt, the FairTax will need advocates on both sides of the fence to see the light of day, and those who want to fashion the FairTax as a Republican-only issue need to think again about such a partisan view. The FairTax is, in my view, a citizen initiative that transcends political affiliation, because to succeed, all are required, and upon enactment, all benefit.

Once the FairTax is through Congress, FairTaxers have little doubt that the same pressure on state legislators from a newly empowered citizenry enjoying the immediate benefits of the FairTax will produce quick results in state-by-state ratification of the constitutional amendment. State legislators, after all, have no stake in the profits and power surrounding the income-tax system. We have seven years to see ratification of repeal of the Sixteenth Amendment. During that time, only the FairTax may be used to collect national revenues. If after seven years the Sixteenth Amendment repeal has not been ratified by the states, the FairTax "sunsets" and disappears so that the two revenue measures may not exist at the same time.

There are, in fact, candidates and elected officials who refuse to support the FairTax by saying that only after the Sixteenth Amendment is repealed will they support it. These are "weasel words" because the overwhelming pressure from the public on state legislators for repeal will likely occur only after citizens are enjoying the advantages of the FairTax. Those who use this dodge typically say they fear that both an income tax and the FairTax will exist together. This reveals a lack of understanding, however, of pending legislation, which holds that if the Sixteenth Amendment is not repealed within seven years, the FairTax sunsets, leaving the country without any tax system.

People often ask me, "What guarantee is there that _____ (fill in a bad outcome caused by congressional self-interest) won't happen?" Simply put, there is no guarantee that Congress and those dependent on the profits from the buying and selling of the tax code will not work mischief. In our republic, there has never been such a guarantee on any public policy except our constitutionally guaranteed rights. It is the absence of our exercise of those rights as voters that allows our taxes to be hidden from us and allows our acceptance of an increasing shift from independence to dependence on government payments and subsidies.

Without informed consent by a majority of voters leading to consequences for the officials who have put us on an unsustainable path of debt, the United States will continue to sink under a growing mountain of public debt. And without an informed citizenry, we will keep in place a destructive and patently unfair taxing system. The FairTax requires, as does our form of government, advanced citizenship. The problem—and the beauty—of self-government is that if we want it to work, *we* must work at it.

Those who have come to expect that our leaders—or someone else—will make this happen or guarantee the policy outcome don't truly understand the nature of a representative democracy. It's understandable, since we, as citizens, seem to find increasing comfort in relying upon those in government for security, leaving ourselves free to live our lives. But after disasters like Hurricane Katrina, the collapse of the savings-and-loan industry, and the government's role in precipitating the 2008 economic crisis, not to mention the almost daily stories of obvious venality, waste, and fraud on the part of government agencies, we should know that it is foolish to rely so heavily on government to take care of us.

Those in Washington have worked to produce a tax system that works quite nicely—and lucratively—for them, even if destructive to the economy and citizens. It is high time that this public policy be made to actually serve the larger public, but to achieve that needed change citizens will have to remember their power and prerogatives under the Constitution. Will it be hard? Yes. Is it worth it to take back control of not only our incomes but our government and our lives? Yes.

Chapter 10   **The Barriers to Good Public Policy**

> "Promote then as an object of primary importance,
> institutions for the general diffusion of knowledge. In
> proportion as the structure of a government gives force
> to public opinion, it is essential that public opinion
> should be enlightened."
>
> —George Washington, Farewell Address, 1796

THE MACHINERY OF elections—the ballots, tabulation protocols, and oversight—has been shown to be vulnerable to manipulation. This is why the 2000 election of George W. Bush had to be decided by the U.S. Supreme Court. Ambiguous ballot choices, voter suppression, missing boxes of ballots, flexible rules on absentee ballots, voter fraud perpetrated by interest groups, and election judges with an agenda have all become part and parcel of our American democracy. One may wonder why—in our age of advanced technology—it is so hard to make voting easy and secure a faithful and accurate count.

The political parties themselves have made independent candidacies all but impossible with onerous requirements at the state level that are designed to maintain a two-party system. Who is served by such barriers? A new class of political elites who have the same characteristics of privilege and rights of royalty that we overturned in the creation of our new republic.

But we have other methods, outside the ballot box, to make our voices heard in exercising our right to "petition the government for a redress of grievances." For most, this means communication with our elected officials. Those who work in grassroots advocacy understand too well that the town-hall meeting held by the local member of Congress is a hit-and-miss affair. Given last year's eruption of citizen passion during the health-care debate, many in Congress fear confrontations with those they represent. There are only a handful in Congress who will still host a town-hall meeting announced more than a week in advance.

We can send e-mails, but a recent study showed that in most cases the representative or senator never sees this correspondence. Hundreds of thousands of e-mails were found unread in elected officials' computer systems. Automatic reply programs generate written responses to e-mails and letters, creating the mere illusion of careful consideration by our elected officials. For citizens to be heard today, they must mount campaigns that employ mass communications tactics, face-to-face visits by the hundreds, if not thousands, and organized letter-writing, phone-call, and other persuasion campaigns that create fear among elected officials that public opinion on a given issue will threaten their chances in the next election. It has become very hard work indeed for the American citizen to enjoy a nation of, by, and for the people, because so many barriers have been created between the citizen and the senator, representative, or president.

For their voices to be heard today, citizens must compete against and overcome those cynical and highly skilled consultants and campaign officials who serve incumbent candidates.

The techniques of winning elections have become so sophisticated that, with few exceptions, incumbents need not worry too much about public-policy initiatives that arise outside the lobbyist/special-interest/advocacy power centers in Washington, D.C. That's because these power elites bring both money and influence to the party and play effectively in the corrupted system of reelecting incumbents.

Incumbent candidates raise money daily. If they serve in a "safe" district that has been gerrymandered to ensure their re-election, they share the money they raise to advance their positions and influence within Congress. If the district is less than safe or a strong challenger emerges, the funds they raise go first to sophisticated polling and market research.

We have come so far and become so sophisticated in this research that a consulting firm can tell the candidate which words work best, how to soften or obscure positions and policies that are disliked by voters, who will likely vote for and against the candidate (down to the make, year, and cost of the voter's family car), and, in general, how to manipulate the body politic to gain the advantage on election day.

Once the "script" has been worked through, the candidate hires a campaign manager, campaign consultant, and fund-raiser who understand the challenges of taking this newly defined and updated image before the voter. Paid advertising is the most direct route, of course, and regardless of what a candidate really believes, a thirty- or sixty-second television message repeated throughout the day can present a compelling image tailored to move voter preferences as defined by the market research.

So what does all this have to do with the FairTax? It's the biggest barrier proponents face in getting the FairTax enacted. When it comes to the ability of Congress to pick winners and losers in the tax code, we find the same hunger for power no matter the ideological image that has been sold to the voting public.

The FairTax was developed far from the halls of power in Washington, D.C. It actually began as market research—similar to the issue polling described above. But this time, instead of trying to determine how best to market a candidate, the goal was to determine the public's preference for a better national tax system. The most common flip answer from those surveyed was to simply eliminate the federal tax system. Most people, however, readily admit, once they get serious, that this would be a terrible mistake. The demands for our pooled money for the common good include our national defense, as well as funding for drug research, food safety, highways and bridges, air-traffic-control systems, social-safety-net programs, and thousands of other programs both worthy and wasteful. Few Americans accept a national model that does not provide for the common good. The question is how to achieve raising needed funds fairly and responsibly.

In a republic, interest groups will always have a say in whether money is spent, in what magnitude, and on what. Let's just accept that as a reality of our system of government. It is the critical judgment of the entire body politic that must be brought to bear so that any single interest group, lobbyist, industry, or special "friend" of those members of Congress who control the public treasury does not enjoy the undue influence that now drives too much policy in both Congress and the White House.

The original market research for the FairTax determined that Americans wanted a tax system that was simple to understand, fair and evenly applied, inexpensive to administer, and free of congressional corruption. Most polled said that they wanted a system that was not onerous to the poor, that did not arbitrarily distort business decisions, and that did not harm the economy.

About $20 million worth of top-level economic research later, the original design of a nonregressive national retail sales tax was completed. In addition, market research identified what most appealed to the voting public. At the top of the list? The right to take home one's entire paycheck, free of automatic deduction of federal withholding and payroll taxes.

There is a way for citizens to regain control of their government, and it is still the ballot box. Despite the sophisticated techniques available to political operatives and the huge sums of money available to candidates for marketing efforts, a well-informed citizenry is capable of seeing through the smoke screens. The trick is first to become well informed and then to hold candidates accountable for their behavior on specific issues, accepting no excuses.

We can also, of course, "petition the government for a redress of grievances" by writing letters, sending faxes, making phone calls, attending town-hall meetings, and visiting with our elected officials. It is not easy. Members of Congress have put as many barriers and staff between us and them as they can. But we chose, fought, and died for a system of government that is anything but easy. Required of us, and long forgotten by most, is our role in directing our government's practices and policies. Between the elections our most powerful tool is our right as citizens to communicate with elected officials.

When enough citizens demand enactment of the FairTax and when enough members of Congress are afraid that they will lose their Washington offices and perks, the FairTax will be enacted. It may require a march of at least a million people on Washington, and it will certainly require a watchful eye during debate and enactment so that amendments are not included that deal tax lobbyists and Congress back into corruption of the tax system—but it can be done when enough Americans speak with one voice and demand change.

Elected officials will be the last converts to the FairTax and will only take up the cause when no other path is open to them except retirement from public service. As one past president remarked to FairTax economists and leaders briefing him on the issue, "You organize the parade and I'll be happy to lead it."

Chapter 11 **The Politics of the FairTax**

"Laws do not persuade just because they threaten."

—Seneca, A.D. 65

DESPITE THE ALMOST universal rejection of the FairTax in Washington, the idea has steadily gained ground among the American people. It remains pending—but without hearings—in Congress, is popularized in best-selling books by Representative John Linder and national talk-show host Neal Boortz, and sees a lot of attention on talk shows and at local meeting halls and in living rooms across the country. The FairTax.org Web site commonly sees millions of visits a year, and former governor Mike Huckabee and other national figures like to occasionally remind the public about the benefits of the idea and legislation. National polls in 2009 examining whether Americans would support a European-type value-added tax (VAT) found almost no support for such a tax *on top* of the income-tax system, but almost half of polled Americans favored a "national sales tax" to *replace* the income tax.

The "FairTax factor" in American politics begins in this case not in the organized campaign efforts of Americans for Fair Taxation but as a word-of-mouth campaign unlike almost any other political movement. It grows in popularity despite resistance from Washington, despite the absence of powerful national allies, and despite being largely ignored or mischaracterized by the national media. In a nutshell it's an "us versus them" social movement as well as a public-policy campaign that, interestingly, inspires an exciting dynamic the farther one travels from the halls of power in Washington.

The 2008 presidential campaign, for example, saw a lot of FairTax activity in early primary states. Executive director David Polyansky, grassroots director Mike Rose, and I, working for Americans for Fair Taxation, reasoned that candidates who had to face real people would be more supportive of the issue precisely because real people generally love the FairTax once they learn about the details of the idea.

We observed that in the cornfields of Iowa and on the back roads of South Carolina, Florida, and New Hampshire, the TV ad is less important than the character and words of the candidate at local campaign stops, coffee shops, and barbershops. Voters in these early primary states like to look into the eyes of candidates and judge them worthy or unworthy. It is one of the healthiest aspects of our presidential races and one constantly criticized and feared by the political elite, including the national media. It was to the places where people congregate that the FairTax campaign took its message, and it was there that candidates started realizing that this issue might have an effect on their political fortunes.

Thus, the FairTax campaign took its show on the road, especially to Iowa, in 2007. An eye-catching FairTax bus toured twenty-six Iowa towns and cities, handing out T-shirts, caps, and information. On the side of the bus, we asked commuters to "Honk if you believe in tax reform" and caused almost continuous noise up and down Iowa's highways and back roads. Journalists received a FairTax "jackalope" with a postcard asking, "Should true tax reform be as mythical as a Jackalope?" It didn't take long for the idea to catch fire, and soon every campaign stop for a presidential candidate saw more and more people showing up with FairTax hats on their heads and FairTax questions on their lips.

Mike Huckabee, the former Arkansas governor and pastor from Hope (the same little town where Bill Clinton grew up), was the first to embrace the FairTax as a central plank of his campaign, and the results shook up the front-runners. Here was an issue that political operatives had not polled!

Huckabee is as nice and decent a man as one will ever meet, an anomaly in politics, to say the least. His friendly demeanor and absence of animosity toward political opponents mask a very sharp intellect and quick grasp of the most complicated foreign and domestic issues. His friendly and open style struck some political operatives and hard-bitten political reporters as "too soft." I believe they judged him too quickly and missed the true measure of the man. I found him to have a sincere connection with the average man and woman, a remarkable intellect, and a vision for the Republican Party that rejected Wall Street for Main Street long before that phrase was embraced by other candidates in the closing days of the election. Agree or disagree with his positions on policies across the board, few, even opponents, deny his honesty, intellect, and decency.

But Huckabee's good nature, moral rectitude, and populist appeal fared poorly when it came to gathering contributions in a field of hard-edged and polished candidates represented by hard-charging political operatives and fund-raisers. It made his underfunded victories in the field all the more remarkable.

When one of the first Republican presidential debates took place in Columbia, South Carolina, Americans for Fair Taxation decided to throw a "Dare to Be Fair" FairTax rally next door. On a Tuesday night about ten thousand people from all over the United States arrived with FairTax banners, hats, and passion. Neal Boortz, Sean Hannity, John Stossel, and others delighted the wildly enthusiastic crowd as a local high-school marching band warmed up offstage. But the most electrifying moment of the night came when Mike Huckabee went onstage and declared that, while the FairTax organization was legally prohibited from endorsing him, *he* enthusiastically endorsed the FairTax. Near pandemonium broke out inside the auditorium.

The crowd shook the walls with applause and cheers. When from the stage I asked the thrilled crowd a few minutes after Huckabee's impromptu speech whether we would eventually have to march on Washington, the roar from the audience was deafening. Every person leaped to their feet, and Neal Boortz, with help from the marching band, led ten thousand chanting and singing FairTaxers out of the auditorium, past the TV broadcast trucks, and around the building next door, where the presidential debate had begun.

The national news media, lined up and down the street with satellite trucks, was caught flat-footed by the unexpected demonstration of passion for the FairTax and reported little on the event. They did what you expect from most and far less than we expect from those who "brake for news." They simply followed the script they had already prepared. The next day the Columbia paper even gave front-page treatment to seven war protesters but failed to mention the ten-thousand-person rally or the energetic march around the debate! Years later the Columbia paper, after bitter and well-founded complaints, did much better with other FairTax rallies.

It was not until months later and only after having seen Fair-Tax crowds gathering at so many campaign stops that George Stephanopoulos at ABC News, hosting yet another nationally televised debate, asked a FairTax question of the Republican candidates. The audience, despite having been warned to be quiet, erupted in applause and cheers—something repeated later in subsequent debates. While the FairTax may not have been much on the radar of many political reporters and editors, it never failed to produce a cheering response from debate audiences and local crowds.

By that time in the long campaign, six of the eight Republican candidates and one Democratic presidential candidate, Mike Gravel, had adopted various statements of support for the Fair-Tax, although both John McCain and Fred Thompson uncomfortably flip-flopped like fish out of water on their support of the FairTax. When it looked like an advantage, they responded to frequent FairTax crowds with statements of support. When political gurus cautioned them, however, they changed their stripes with statements that blurred their views, saying the Fair-Tax was "a good start."

Huckabee went on to the win the Iowa caucus, shocking pollsters, pundits, and operatives that his underfunded campaign could best front-runner Mitt Romney and better-known John McCain. No, the FairTax campaign never asked a single person to vote for Huckabee. We actually said and ran ads stating that the *FairTax* was the best candidate for real change, even if not a candidate. Huckabee caught the FairTax lightning, leaving Romney to get burned by it, because Huck took a positive stand on a position voters favored. He later finished strongly, although he did not win, in South Carolina, Florida, and Georgia. Most national pundits attributed his successes to Christian Right voters, certainly part of his appeal, but ignored the "FairTax factor."

The *Wall Street Journal*, on the other hand, as well as an influential group of politically active, megawealthy Republicans called the Club for Growth, saw someone in their favored candidate's way and began to demonize him and, in the case of the *Journal* and other conservative publications, the FairTax.

In an embarrassing and revealing departure from its normally staid and restrictive filters on guest editorials, the *Journal* allowed Washington tax lobbyist Bruce Bartlett to write a rambling and venomous piece describing the FairTax as an invention of the Church of Scientology and then, for almost a month, refused to allow a response piece by FairTax founder Leo Linbeck—a devout Catholic.

About that time the influential and well-funded millionaires' Club for Growth began a series of articles and TV and radio ads describing former governor Huckabee as a "tax and spend" man for his record in Arkansas, where the state constitution requires an annually balanced budget and where legislators preferred to raise taxes for education instead of cutting already starved school budgets or going into federal court.

The Iowa vote for Huckabee scared tax lobbyists because they understood better than most political analysts the potential of the FairTax to not only affect political fortunes but threaten their lucrative practices. In subsequent weeks and months, the wagons were circled in Washington, with the *National Review*, an icon of conservative thought, opining that the FairTax was a disaster for Republicans, not because it lacked merit necessarily, but because it was too easily distorted by Democrats—and because it was unlikely the public could ever overcome the self-interest of those very power brokers and legislators the magazine editors routinely lunch with. With this perspective at work, Bartlett found even more ink for his distortions of the FairTax and his insulting and obvious disdain for the ordinary Americans who embraced it.

This conservative perspective has taken its toll at the highest levels of Republican politics in Washington, D.C. Distressingly, Representative Pete Sessions, who heads the National Republican Congressional Committee, makes no bones about advising candidates to avoid congressional cosponsorship of the pending legislation rather than learning more about the issue in order to become a forceful champion. Such a big idea, no matter how fundamentally worthy, is thought too risky by Mr. Sessions and others. The road back to Republican majorities, according to many in Washington, is not built on new, forceful ideas but on criticism of the policies of Barack Obama and Democrats in Congress. It is a negative strategy built on division rather than a positive path that puts faith in the ability of the American people to discern the right course for the nation. Instead of leading, it is a "sniper" approach that avoids embracing the big ideas that are so needed to solve the really big problems that hurt the nation. The desire to avoid any political risk undermines real debate or distinct policy choices and ill serves both the political process and the American voter.

FairTax economists and experts did brief Obama campaign economic advisers on the FairTax and had great hopes that these seemingly receptive and interested experts had seen its clear advantages not only to the country but to Democratic voters. So much of Mr. Obama's hopeful message about throwing off the influence of lobbyists and special interests and bringing tax relief and hope to millions of Americans seemed to define the very essence of the Fair Tax that it was perhaps natural that FairTax advocates perceived progress with his economic advisers. Those hopes were never realized in the Obama campaign, however, and all campaign-trail talk about taxes by Mr. Obama, Hillary Clinton, and other Democratic presidential candidates (besides former Alaska senator Mike Gravel) focused on repeal of George W. Bush's tax breaks for upper-income Americans. When it came to real tax reform the Democratic campaigns adopted the same strategy as I've heard from Republican operatives—just criticize the other side, and play the class warfare arguments for all they are worth.

As President Obama has taken on the daunting challenges of the economy and his ambitious agenda for fundamental change in policy, the tax lobbyists have remained untouched in their lucrative and influential roles in Washington, D.C. Mr. Obama's policies have dramatically increased the nation's debt and the obligations of coming generations of Americans to government. Whether greater dependency on government and far larger debt obligations are the right course is an issue for the American people to decide in an honest debate that puts the real truths on the table for all to see.

I liked Mr. Obama's campaign of hope and the recruitment of so many previously disaffected Americans into the political system because basically, I believe that the real answers to our many problems and unrealized national potential live, largely untapped, in the American people and their participation in the political system, not in the self-interested ideas of the political elite who span the political spectrum from left to right. That admiration, however, has been tempered in me by his unwillingness to take on the badly corrupted tax system. One hopes that grassroots Democrats and Americans of every political belief will still inspire a change of perspective in Mr. Obama.

Today, Democratic campaign organizations in Washington like the FairTax because they find it an easy weapon against those who embrace it. In this the *National Review* writers were proved correct in their fear that the issue could be turned against a candidate. It is easily and willingly distorted and will continue to be until average Americans are as familiar with the truth as are FairTax advocates and until candidates do the necessary homework and stand up to forcefully and defiantly answer such politically inspired attacks. The other explanation for political exploitation of the FairTax by Democratic campaign organizations is more difficult. The FairTax campaign itself is seen by most news organizations and many in the public as a conservative and Republican effort, and every FairTax rally burnishes this image. Those who draw the crowds to these events, such as Neal Boortz and Mike Huckabee and Sean Hannity, have done as much as anyone to educate the public on the FairTax but are clearly *not* Democrats, and press reports fairly characterize these events as thrilling conservative-minded crowds.

Local FairTax supporters find it hard not to be attracted to large gatherings with such conservative stars but in truth, Fair-Taxers need to be attending Green Party events, teacher meetings, senior-citizen clubs, and local union meetings, which often desire outside speakers. This is, after all, an *American* movement that, unusually, can bring Left and Right together.

Only recently have locally known Democratic/Obama field organizers like Jessica Wexler stood before large crowds to declare that they, too, believe in the FairTax as a solution for all of America, blue and red. Jessica is right when she says that we can disagree about what our money is spent on but still agree on how it can be better collected.

This is the unrealized potential of the FairTax movement,

and it requires the difficult step of setting aside the partisan passions that keep conservatives and liberals from listening to one another. It is only by bringing together both ideologies and all of us who fall in between that the FairTax will eventually be enacted.

Some—especially those who thrive on disdain for our fellow citizens—would say that it is impossible. I disagree and remember very well the unity that swept the nation on the heels of the 9/11 attacks. When motivated, we have pulled together as an American family that includes an amazing diversity of backgrounds, talents, origins, and beliefs. We often forget how much strength, decency, and common sense really exist in our great experiment that allows such American diversity. Our arguments about everything else will inevitably go on as they always have—it's healthy—but this is an issue where we can join together to correct destructive public policy and, together, create something better.

The frustrating problem with gaining widespread public acceptance of the FairTax, however, boils down to both perception and polarization. Because most current congressional cosponsors are Republican and nearly every nationally recognized advocate is conservative, many other citizens with different political viewpoints will not even take the time to consider whether the idea might actually have merit. We have become so polarized between "red" and "blue" states and between conservative and progressive ideologies that "big ideas" circulated by either side almost never get more than short shrift or reflexive knee-jerk criticism by the other side.

Big ideas become, instead, ammunition for those dedicated to dividing us to win elections. Mr. Sessions, heading the National Republican Congressional Committee, is both cowardly *and* politically practical. He sees the Democratic National Committee, the Democratic Congressional Campaign Committee, and the Democratic Senatorial Campaign Committee routinely funding television and direct-mail campaign advertising accusing FairTax-supporting candidates of wanting "a new 23% tax on everything!" You have to be grateful that those who wrote the Constitution were made of sterner stuff or we might have merely won the right to vote for Members of Parliament by now.

The attack ads never mention that the new tax system will also allow wage earners to take home their whole paychecks or that it will eliminate all federal taxes on savings, investment, and, indeed, upward mobility. Few attacked candidates or Republican counterparts to these national Democratic campaign committees, with the exception of Mike Huckabee, have ever even tried to talk with voters about how the FairTax can save American jobs or take the heavy burden of the regressive FICA tax off the shoulders of the poor. The most common reaction by those attacked has been to duck and cover. Surprised? Let's remember that cowardice in politics is exactly why John F. Kennedy's *Profiles in Courage*, which details courageous political acts, is such a very thin little book.

Many FairTax candidates and elected officials don't seem to have either the knowledge or the strength of will to forcefully denounce such distortions. Because the national FairTax campaign is nonpartisan, has no political action committee, and does not endorse candidates and because it is a relatively cash-poor campaign, such attacks are almost never answered with sufficient bandwidth by Americans for Fair Taxation to offset the damage. While the original thought to avoid a FairTax Political Action Committee may very well need to be reexamined, the perhaps too innocent belief was that rather than taking political sides, the issue would naturally appeal to candidates on both sides of the aisle because of its clear merits. For many in politics this is the kind of weakness that can be easily exploited.

Seeing that the FairTax campaign was not positioned to run millions of dollars of ads in defense of the FairTax and absent a well-funded political action committee, the *Wall Street Journal's* editorial page, as well as the *National Review* and others, reacted with great indignation to Mike Huckabee's winning the Iowa presidential caucus. They saw that voters in Iowa were attracted to Huckabee's position on the FairTax, allowing him to win against Mitt Romney when Romney had outspent him dozens of times over. They, like the conservative *National Journal*, warned that the issue was too easily distorted by opponents to be embraced nationally. Their skepticism about a needed change that is nevertheless unpopular with the political elite and underdefended with the now common million-dollar media budget is just one problem with the politics of the FairTax.

Many members of the Washington establishment, including the campaign apparatuses of both parties, tax advocacy groups, tax lobbyists, scholars who are invested in the income-tax system, and even many "independent" pundits, have attacked the FairTax idea. Others just ignore it. Outside Washington, even conservative boat rocker Rush Limbaugh refuses to have any FairTax advocates on his daily radio show. One of his producers once quipped to a FairTax talent booker, Jason McKinley, that Rush "has no interest in helping Neal Boortz [another national radio talk host and author of books on the FairTax] sell any more books." On the air, Limbaugh has given the FairTax short shrift, dismissing the idea as "politically unrealistic." In this, even Limbaugh, champion of conservatives, paradoxically doubts the ability of the American people to overcome Washington's bipartisan self-interest in the income-tax system. Sean Hannity, also on the right, likes the FairTax and has both attended and covered several rallies but is sometimes scolded on the air by listeners who don't feel that he gives the issue much airtime even during shows that focus on tax policy.

Doubtless vexing to defenders of the income-tax system is the dogged durability of the FairTax cause and its enduring and growing popularity. The issue just won't go away, despite the determined efforts of powerful voices in Washington to distort the genesis of the idea, the effects of the FairTax on tax burdens and government revenues, and the FairTax rate. Every new attack seems to strengthen the resolve of hometown advocates who rail against the industry that has grown up around the tax code and the workings of the tax-writing committees in Washington. Groups supporting the FairTax have popped up on social networking sites like Facebook and Twitter, Harley motorcycle clubs have initiated "freedom rides" for the FairTax, YouTube videos abound, rallies see thousands of participants, and talk radio has devoted hundreds of shows and thousands of hours to the subject. It is a simmering cauldron of hope, resentment, and citizen passion.

Advocates believe that despite steep political challenges to enactment, the FairTax has the potential and magnitude of effect to immediately reverse the economic crisis. And swimming against the polarized tide of the day, many FairTax advocates believe that the issue has the potential to bring the political Right and Left together against the corrupted tax system.

Because so much top-level economic research on the FairTax is available to the public and because books by Boortz and Linder have been so popular, hometown advocates have become experts on both the basic concepts and the advanced research underlying the FairTax proposal. A growing number of average citizens now quickly recognize false claims and distortions by critics. They complain that pundits haven't read the books and routinely misstate the elements of the proposal either out of lack of homework or because it is unthinkable to their D.C. friends. They recognize that rich and powerful tax lobbyists will do and say anything to protect the billion-dollar K Street tax lobbying industry and that congressional tax-writing committees are addicted to the power to corrupt the tax code with profit- and power-driven perks for the favored few.

Chapter 12 **What You Can Do—and What Others Are Doing**

> "Never doubt that a small group of thoughtful, committed citizens can change the world. Indeed, it is the only thing that ever has."
>
> —Margaret Mead

L ET'S START WITH Houstonians Jack Trotter, Bob McNair (owner of the NFL's Houston Texans), and FairTax chairman Leo Linbeck and their friends as examples of what people determined to make a difference can do. It started at a weekly lunch when the three were comparing notes about the vagaries and injustices of the tax code. Remarkably, that casual conversation turned into determination to actually do something about it. These men, older and very successful, contributed or raised more than $22 million for the research that underpins the Fair-Tax concept. They were not motivated by selfish or narrow interest—each does very well with tax accountants and attorneys under the current system. They developed the FairTax proposal as a gift to their country because they wanted to leave something behind greater than themselves. As hard as it is to accept, such people do still exist.

There just is not enough room to thank everyone but I'll try to cover those I know best. There is Kenan Pollack of the Internet consulting company Convio in Austin, Texas, who has gone far beyond paid consultant status with his creativity, e-cards, ads, Web promotions, and "Energizer bunny," never-say-die attitude. Special heartfelt thanks go to Karen Walby, an accomplished Florida economist central to the national FairTax movement. Aaron Schutte, a longtime FairTax front-desk worker, has actually answered more questions, fielded more phone calls, and posted more material on the Web about the FairTax than anyone else in the country. He is yet another valuable but largely unsung hero, as is the man who first explained the FairTax to tens of thousands—Tom Wright of Florida.

Longtime FairTax consultant and former chief of staff to Representative Dick Armey, Denis Calabrese, brings eloquence and quiet common sense to the needed effort. Recent additions to the FairTax effort, Bill and Kari Butcher, are contributing a genius for public policy marketing work to the national campaign that promises to finally put the effort on high-speed rails. The public has also come to know about the FairTax and has met many FairTax volunteers on the air because of the tireless work of Jason McKinley at Americans for Fair Taxation. Amazingly, Jason has booked more than eight hundred shows in a little over thirty-six months. He is something of a phenom even among passionate FairTaxers.

Beyond these hardworking people lies a large volunteer effort that has driven the FairTax in our hometowns. Gene Keyes and Lloyd Newsome of Georgia and Floridian Mark Gupton have each adopted sophisticated grassroots organizing strategies. Michael Frederick of South Dakota and his wife, Kelley, in Alabama are longtime and effective leaders. In Georgia, Neal Boortz's home, extensive knowledge of the FairTax is so common that an ill-considered Democratic Senatorial Campaign Committee TV blitz against FairTax sponsor Senator Saxby Chambliss actually backfired badly on the Democratic candidate, who was forced to renounce the ads. Up-and-coming Georgia gubernatorial candidate John Oxendine is running on the FairTax. Oxendine wants each state to pass a legislative "memorial" demanding a constitutional convention to repeal the Sixteenth Amendment.

Bill Rollyson, a FairTax intellectual and longtime regional director has mentored many in West Virginia and beyond and has done much to build organizing strength. Bill has gone to bat with the smartest critics in the country and proved them wrong using FairTax research. The eloquent and courtly former Missouri lieutenant governor, Bill Phelps, has appeared on talk shows, in speeches, and in meetings with citizens throughout Missouri. Jack Jackson, the South Carolina volunteer state director, has worked hard to host rallies and organize new supporters face-to-face and through his Web site. Danny and Donna Higgins in Indiana are young, internet savvy, and committed. Jim Bennett in New Jersey has been the lynchpin of the New Jersey efforts for years with a level-headed and steady approach. Roger Buchholtz of Michigan keeps the idea growing there where the FaxTax offers hope to the unemployed. Barry Hickley, a high-tech entrepreneur in Massachusetts has advanced the FairTax with key congressional Democrats and friends alike. Always cheerful and optimistic, Marilyn Rickert in Chicago, Bill Spillane in California, Lori Klein in Arizona, Jim Tomasik on Fair-TaxNation.com, and hundreds of others have done truly amazing work as leaders of an almost all-volunteer effort.

And then there are the talk show hosts themselves and their shows—the new venue for average Americans who, unlike the misunderstood, earnest, and honestly populist Joe (the Plumber) Wurzelbacher (also a FairTaxer), almost never get their moment in the national spotlight. Radio Hall of Famer Neal Boortz, of course, is the most dedicated and constant champion of the FairTax with a national bullhorn. But in cities across the country, other hosts have added their voices. This book is too small to list them all, but here are just a few of the very best: Spud McConnell (WWL, New Orleans), Martha Zoller (WDUN, Gainesville, Georgia), Rocky D (WTMA, Charleston, South Carolina), Jan Mickelson (WHO, Des Moines, Iowa), Tom Roten (WVHU, Huntington, West Virginia), David Vincent Jericho (KSGF, Springfield, Missouri), Raubin Pierce (WIBW, Topeka, Kansas), and Lynn Woolley (KTEM, Temple, Texas). Each has enthusiastically featured the FairTax, sometimes with a good degree of healthy skepticism but always with a hunger for citizen-inspired improvement of destructive and top-down public policies.

But How About the Rest of Us?

The self-interest of Washington in keeping the income-tax system going is so strong that it will take an all-hands-on-deck attitude by Americans to overturn that system. Fortunately, the Founding Fathers anticipated that even our government would concentrate more and more power unto itself, and they provided us with the tools to correct the corruption that is inherent in any form of government. If you've never done it before, have some fun working to make your government yours again.

Many of the tools and most of the information needed by interested volunteers can be found at FairTax.org. The Web site contains the beginning of a list of state and local organizations, social networking sites, and communication links to members of Congress. There is a FairTax calculator that allows each taxpayer to examine his or her own tax burden under the FairTax and, most important, a wealth of research examining almost every aspect of how the FairTax will affect individual taxpayers, income groups, and the economy of the nation.

To join the growing FairTax citizen army in your congressional district or hometown, just step up to the plate. Make up your mind that you can make a difference—and you will. The first step is arming yourself with the research—and armoring yourself against both common misunderstandings and deliberate distortions. Be generous with fellow citizens about misunderstandings and relentless about deliberate distortions. This book, in truth, only scratches the surface, but the research is at FairTax.org for all to see.

Once so armed and armored, make your voice heard. What can you do to help promote the FairTax? Start by writing a letter to your representative and your two senators. Find their positions on the FairTax legislation at FairTax.org. When you get the inevitable "Washington speak" letter back, don't give up!

Challenge the vague assumptions or outright distortions with the truth. Write more letters and politely but firmly ask for a reasoned response. Forget about e-mails, because too many offices, as I have described, simply never read them. Type letters, or even better, put together a simple handwritten note. What you are after is the rarest of things these days between government and citizen—clarity. Share what you learn online or drop a note to the FairTax campaign—it will help.

Now that you've tuned up your advocacy with your members of Congress—yes, they are supposed to be "yours"—write a letter to your president. Write to Mr. Obama and remind him that he promised to take government away from the lobbyists but that more than half of all the Washington lobbying dollars are still spent on the tax code. Tell him that the FairTax can heal America's economy, is good for every income group, and ends the corruption that he promised us would end. Better yet, formulate your own good reason to support the FairTax. Be respectful of the office, but firmly ask for specific answers to your letter.

And don't forget that every congressional office in Washington and back home, every committee and subcommittee and the White House, has phones. The congressional switchboard number in Washington is (202) 224-3121. The White House operators are at (202) 456-1400. Rage, no matter how sincerely felt, won't get you very far. The operators at Congress and the White House are very nice people who take a lot of grief they don't deserve, so cut them a break. As American citizens equal in the eyes of the Constitution with every elected official, you don't have to bow or curtsy, of course, but take the high road even with snippy and self-important congressional staffers who never learned or have forgotten the true role of the citizen in our government.

Take it another step by writing a letter to your local paper's editor or to a national publication. Short and sweet is the usual rule. Be sure to include your name, address, and phone number so they can confirm that you wrote the letter. Ready to really write and let loose? Make it short for Twitter, make it funny and compelling for Facebook, make a funny or dramatic video and post it on YouTube. There are now literally hundreds and hundreds of social network sites aimed at different audiences that range from stay-at-home moms to financial sites to the highly political. Bring the FairTax message to each with an explanation of how this idea can help each.

Call in to the local or national talk show host who doesn't really believe that the American people can overcome the political class. Get comfortable, set aside some time, and start calling (and redialing) in to a show (it takes a lot of patience to get past the busy signal). Be ready to be turned down by the screeners of shows whose hosts don't want to talk about the FairTax. Yes, it's frustrating, but when the number of callers asking the same thing reaches a certain tipping point, you will find yourself on the air and your voice will be heard. In this way, for a precious moment or two you become the champion and voice of a true citizen movement.

Those with an even greater passion to see the FairTax create jobs and save the economy can organize a local chapter of FairTaxers. Develop a speech and take it to seniors' clubs, Rotaries, Kiwanis, chambers of commerce, and Democratic and Republican clubs. Have materials and ask for names and e-mails that can be added on to the FairTax.org database.

Start a Web site, start a FairTax club devoted to daily blogging on social networking sites, or get together with others to create compelling or compellingly funny videos for YouTube, as Paul Wizikowski did recently when he produced a heartfelt personal statement on how the FairTax is really about the American dream. Draw a circle that encompasses rather than excludes.

Are you a college student? The FairTax needs campus clubs and advocates. It is a huge, unrealized potential of the FairTax movement and wide open for you to make a difference—and make your mark. You build it and people will come to the FairTax field of dreams. Speakers are available, and if there is any generation that deserves relief from the unfair debt being put on their shoulders, it is yours. When I was in college, we believed we could change the world. We didn't change it as much as we hoped, but our passion for self-determination and a new direction was nevertheless healthy and very much in keeping with our Founding Fathers' vision of an active and involved citizenry. Spark that passion again against corruption in our own government that hurts you and every other American. I guess I'm dating myself but I still think Bob Dylan had it right when he sang "The Times They Are a-Changin'," which inspired so many to try to make a difference. Please update this old warhorse's favorite music with the current sounds that inspire the same sentiment for healthy and needed citizen leadership. You either inherit a difficult and dwindling future or work now to create something far better.

Senior citizen? There is simply no good reason that our society treats those who retire as ghosts. Casting aside the aged is nothing short of national stupidity. You were needed and valuable before you retired, and in reality, you still are. Use the time on your hands to make our government work properly again. Your experience and wisdom in making it this far in life, adapting to all the challenges of a lifetime, and building families and communities could not be more needed by your country than it is right now. Embrace the idea that we owe a better world to those who follow us and that we have common American cause with our children and grandchildren. I promise you this is an investment of time that pays back more than is given.

Perhaps most important, whatever your age, hector your elected officials at every opportunity. Don't let them ignore you. Go to town-hall meetings and campaign events, and when asked to support a politician, ask for their support for the FairTax. If they won't represent you and the best interests of the nation, don't help them with your vote or your money. Make that stance crystal clear at every chance. Be the squeaky wheel.

Speaking of campaign money, the forever-starved FairTax organization deserves a few of your dollars. Help it. Online contribution forms are available, and there's no need to worry that your hard-earned dollars are going to pay for high overhead. The office is in a tiny, free space, the organization has a minuscule paid staff, and it counts and spends every penny as if it were the last one. If you like "lean and mean" in a national organization, you'll love Americans for Fair Taxation at FairTax.org.

Finally

There are very few political or public-policy causes that can have greater impact than the FairTax. For individuals across the political and income spectrum, no single legislative act can deliver as much needed relief. For that matter, few issues have such potential to finally unite the American people on the left, right, and center behind a single cause. For the national economy, nothing can deliver so much improvement in such a short period of time. For restoration of the noble experiment in self-government that was created in 1776, there is nothing as effective or as needed in restoring the relationship between citizen and government.

It all comes down to citizenship. For a rising standard of living that helps every interconnected American, the FairTax creates a rising sea that lifts all boats. If we truly desire a nation based on opportunity and personal freedom rather than government control of our lives and our pursuit of happiness, we must use the power still invested in us under our form of government to bring our real fiscal issues into the open. That means practicing advanced citizenship to control our government and ensure our freedoms—our Founding Fathers never promised us anything more.

What are you waiting for? It won't get better without you. It's time to get busy.

ACKNOWLEDGMENTS

I AM NOT an economist or a historian but I have borrowed heavily from both in writing this book and owe much to all those in the Notes section of this book and quoted in these pages. For all the economists who worked tirelessly to construct, defend, and advance the FairTax with scholarly research, thank you.

To Leo Linbeck at Americans for Fair Taxation and all those who put themselves in the lion's den by having the nerve to suggest our tax system is badly broken and for developing something so much better—including Dan Mastromarco, David Burton, and Karen Walby—thank you.

I want to thank those at the Tax Foundation and those at the Center for Responsive Politics for their outstanding work to shine light, through research, on the reality of the tax system and the effect of money on public policy.

To John Linder, thank you for having the courage and vision to champion the FairTax, to speak so eloquently about it, and to hold your course even though you serve on the House Ways and Means Committee that is at the center of all the problems with the current tax system.

To Brooke Carey, my editor extraordinaire, and all those at Sentinel, thank you for your almost entirely patient help guiding this first-time author. You drove me when I needed a kick, kept me on track with encouragement when I felt overwhelmed by all the other demands on my time, and held my hand when so much work was lost in a computer mishap.

Finally, while writing this book I occasionally bumped heads, hard, with passionate FairTax grassroots leaders who hold very different views of how to advance the FairTax campaign. From those sometimes heated discussions I found even more inspiration to write this book because even in disagreement over tactics and strategies, I came to honor their passion, commitment, and sometimes lonely dedication to the cause. It is an American cause populated by the same wonderful, maddening mix of backgrounds and viewpoints that represents the true strength of this nation. Thank you to each and every one who work so hard for a better future for our country.

NOTES

3 **In 2008 *USA Today* reported:** Dennis Cauchon, "Leap in U.S. Debt Hits Taxpayers with 12% More Red Ink," *USA Today*, May 5, 2009.

17 **Effective FairTax Rate [chart]:** Americans for Fair Taxation, "About the FairTax," FairTax.org, developed by Karen Walby for Americans for Fair Taxation, Karen Walby, Ph.D., February 16, 2009, http://www.fairtax.org/site/PageServer?pagename=about_faq_answers#5.

19 **Stability of the Tax Base [chart]:** Americans for Fair Taxation, "About the FairTax," FairTax.org, http://www.fairtax.org/site/PageServer?pagename=about_faq_answers#5.

22 **The 2009 FairTax Prebate Schedule [chart]:** Americans for Fair Taxation, "About the FairTax," http://www.fairtax.org/site/PageServer?pagename=about_faq_answers#3.

24 **A study by the Government Accountability Office:** United States Government Accountability Office, "Cost of the Income Tax System," in *Tax Policy: Estimates of the Costs of the Federal Tax System* (Washington, D.C.: United States Government Accountability Office, August 2005).

24 **The FairTax will provide needed medicine:** Alan Auerbach, "Tax Reform, Capital Allocation, Efficiency, and Growth," in Henry Aaron and William Gale, eds., *Economic Effects of Fundamental Tax Reform* (Washington, D.C.: Brookings Institution Press, 1996), p. 58; Dale W. Jorgenson, "The Economic Impact of the National Retail Sales Tax" (Final Report to Americans for Fair Taxation), May 18, 1997, as presented to the U.S. House of Representatives, http://linderfairtax.house.gov/index.cfm?Fuse

Action=Files.View&FileStore_id=18. Retrieved 2008-02-20; Laurence J. Kotlikoff, "The Economic Impact of Replacing Federal Income Taxes with a Sales Tax," Cato Institute, Policy Analysis No. 193, April 15, 1993; Laurence J. Kotlikoff, "Replacing the U.S. Federal Tax System with a Retail Sales Tax— Macroeconomic and Distributional Impacts," Report to Americans for Fair Taxation, December 1996; Gary and Aldona Robbins, "Looking Back to Move Forward: What Tax Policy Costs Americans and the Economy," Institute for Policy Innovation, Policy Report No. 127, September 1, 1994.

25 **By year ten, employment in the United States:** Arduin, Laffer & Moore Econometrics, "A Macroeconomic Analysis of the FairTax Proposal," July 2006.

25 **Cumulative Growth in Employment, Take-Home Wages [chart]:** Arduin, Laffer & Moore Econometrics, "A Macroeconomic Analysis of the FairTax Proposal."

30 **Many experts predict an almost immediate $10–15 trillion:** While there are no definitive studies on how much greater investment in the United States would be after enactment of the FairTax, the combination of estimates of American wealth now offshore and the effect on foreign corporations attracted to the U.S. market without taxes on manufacturing and production make Representative John Linder's estimate of $11 trillion or more of new investment in the U.S. economy reasonable. Estimates of just American wealth now held offshore can be found at http://www.globalpolicy.org/component/content/article/214/44193.html.

31 **Here is a snapshot of the major findings:** David G. Tuerck, Jonathan Haughton, Keshab Bhattari, et al., "The Economic Effects of the FairTax: Results from the Beacon Hill Institute CGE Model," Beacon Hill Institute at Suffolk University, Boston, February 2007 (available at http://www.fairtax.org/site/PageServer?pagename=about_BHI_0607).

32 **Summary of the Effects of the FairTax [chart]:** Paul Bachman, Jonathan Haughton, Laurence J. Kotlikoff, et al., "Taxing Sales Under the FairTax: What Rate Works?" *Tax Notes*, November 13, 2006.

33 **Dale Jorgenson, an economist at Harvard:** Dale W. Jorgenson, "The Economic Impact of the National Retail Sales Tax," for Americans for Fair Taxation, November 1996 (findings available within White Paper at http://www.fairtax.org/PDF/TheFairTaxAndEconomicGrowth.pdf).

36 **Actual Cost of Purchasing a New Car (chart):** Americans for Fair Taxation, "The FairTax Lowers the Cost of a New U.S. Produced Automobile," FairTax.org, http://www.fairtax.org/PDF/TheFairTaxlowersthecostofUSautomobiles-110206.pdf. See also Jerry Hausman, "Hausman Study Shows Distortions in International Trading System Hurting U.S. Manufacturers: An Economic Analysis of WTO Rules on Border Adjustability of Taxes," May 2006.

38 **Compliance costs are so high:** Scott A. Hodge, J. Scott Moody, and Wendy P. Warcholik, "The Rising Cost of Complying with the Federal Income Tax," Tax Foundation Special Report 138, January 2006; J. Scott Moody, "The Cost of Complying with the Federal Income Tax," Tax Foundation Special Report 112, 2002.

38 **This "tax gap," or money owed:** About.com: US Government Info, "What Is the Tax Gap and Why Does It Cost You Money?" http://usgovinfo.about.com/od/smallbusiness/a/taxgap.htm.

43 **According to one recent study by three:** Raquel Meyer Alexander, Stephen Mazza, and Susan Scholz, "Measuring Rates of Return on Lobbying Expenditures: An Empirical Case Study of Tax Breaks for Multinational Corporations," 29 *Journal of Law and Politics* (forthcoming 2010). The study was conducted by Raquel Meyer Alexander, assistant professor of accounting; Stephen Mazza, associate dean of the school of law; and Susan

Scholz, associate professor of accounting and Harper Faculty Fellow, and was presented at the Critical Tax Theory Conference, sponsored by the Indiana University Maurer School of Law in Bloomington.

43 **One of the authors of the study:** Dan Eggen, "Investments Can Yield More on K Street, Study Indicates," *Washington Post*, April 12, 2009.

44 **As tax lawyer and financial blogger:** Hale Stewart, "Why Our Tax Code Is So Complicated," The Huffington Post, April 13, 2009.

48 **With at least $75,000 a year:** Jeffrey Rohaly, Leonard E. Burman, Matthew Hall, et al., "Key Points on the Alternative Minimum Tax," Urban-Brookings Tax Policy Center, January 21, 2004 (available at http://www.brookings.edu/opinions/2004/0121feder albudget_burman.aspx).

57 **Writing in the *Nebraska Law Review*:** Cheryl D. Block, "Congress and Accounting Scandals: Is the Pot Calling the Kettle Black?" *Nebraska Law Review*, Vol. 82, 2003, p. 365.

73 **After the poor, the greatest:** Laurence J. Kotlikoff, "The Fair-Tax and Middle Americans—A Case Study," January 20, 2008 (available at http://www.fairtax.org/PDF/TheFairTaxAnd MiddleAmericans—CaseStudy.pdf).

73 **In 2008 the brilliant Boston University economist:** Laurence J. Kotlikoff and David Rapson, "Comparing Average and Marginal Tax Rates Under the FairTax and the Current System of Federal Taxation," National Bureau of Economic Research Working Paper No. W11831, December 2005, revised October 2006, with John Diamond, Jane Gravelle, and Peter Mieszkowski.

83 **When one blogger confronted:** The blogger was Jason Mattera, whose blog is at JasonMattera.com. You can view a video clip of the incident at http://www.youtube.com/watch?v=rdtFW CrCh0s.

83 **"While over the years"**: *U.S.News and World Report*, Sam Dealey, October 4, 2009.

85 **"Hundreds of former members"**: Interview with Dave Levinthal, communication director, the Center for Responsive Politics.

85 **Among many others, Vin Weber**: Kim Eisler, "Hired Guns: The City's 50 Top Lobbyists," *Washington.com*, June 1, 2007.

88 **Even before landing those dream lobbying jobs**: Legistorm, "House Ways and Means Committee Staff Salaries," October 2009, http://www.legistorm.com/office/House_Ways_and_Means_Committee/1438/60.html.

94 **As Harvard economists Edward L. Glaeser**: Edward L. Glaeser and Jesse M. Shapiro, "The Benefits of the Home Mortgage Interest Deduction," Harvard Institute Research Working Paper No. 1979, October 2002.

94 **As Roger Lowenstein brilliantly observed**: Roger Lowenstein, "Who Needs the Mortgage-Interest Deduction?" *New York Times*, March 5, 2006.

96 **"True Cost" of Housing [chart]**: Several economic studies have estimated that switching from an income-tax system to a consumption-tax system such as the FairTax would result in an interest-rate drop of approximately 25 percent. See, e.g., John E. Golob, "How Would Tax Reform Affect Financial Markets?" *Economic Review*, Federal Reserve Bank of Kansas City, fourth quarter, 1995 (http://www.fairtax.org/PDF/PromotingHome Ownership.pdf).

97 **According to a study conducted**: David G. Tuerck, Jonathan Haughton, Alfonso Sanchez-Penalver, et al., "The FairTax and Charitable Giving," Beacon Hill Institute at Suffolk University, Boston, February 2007. See also John S. Barry, "Faith, Growth, and Charity," *Policy Review*, March 1977. ("The most overwhelming proof that tax incentives have a relatively minor effect on individual charity is the tremendous consistence over time of giving as a percentage of income. Although the tax code

has changed frequently and dramatically over the past 23 years, giving as a share of personal income has hovered around 1.83%. This measure reached as high as 1.95% in 1989 and as low as 1.71% in 1985. The narrow range has persisted even though the top marginal tax rate has fluctuated in that period between 28 and 70 percent. It suggests that raising income growth will do more to boost charitable giving than any tax incentive.")

101 **many FairTax advocates have misunderstood**: Dale W. Jorgenson, "The Economic Impact of the National Retail Sales Tax," Report to Americans for Fair Taxation, May 18, 1997.

105 **falsely attribute the genesis of the FairTax:** Bruce Bartlett, "FairTax, Flawed Tax," *Wall Street Journal*, August 26, 2007 (available at http://www.opinionjournal.com/extra/?id= 110010523). See also Laurence J. Kotlikoff, "Why the FairTax Will Work: A Response to Bartlett," *Tax Notes*, February 4, 2008 (available at http://www.fairtax.org/PDF/080115-Kotlikoff_on_Barlett.pdf).

INDEX